ELEMENTARY TRAINING FOR MUSICIANS

Elementary Training for Musicians

By

By
PAUL HINDEMITH

Second Edition
Revised 1949

SCHOTT & CO. LTD. LONDON

48 Great Marlborough Street London W1V 2BN

B. Schott's Söhne, Mainz–
Schott Music Corporation, New York

SOLE DISTRIBUTOR IN THE U.S. AND CANADA:
European American Music Distributors Corporation
Valley Forge, Pennsylvania

ISBN 0-901938-16-5
Copyright © 1946 by B. Schott's Söhne, Mainz
Copyright © renewed 1974
All rights for the U.S., Canada, and Mexico controlled exclusively by
European American Music Distributors Corporation

CONTENTS

(For complete references, see INDEX*)*

CONTENTS—*Continued*

PREFACE

The music student entering a class in harmony is in general insufficiently prepared with respect to basic principles—governing Rhythm, Meter, Intervals, Scales, Notation—and their correct application. In all phases of his teaching, the harmony teacher has to face the fact that his students have no solid foundation to build upon. There is little doubt that, save in a few exceptional cases, the methods by which those basic principles are taught are deplorable. Most musicians pick up what they know of these things at random, along with their accumulating knowledge of more "practical" musical matters. Others do go through courses in Elementary Training, but in general these courses provide hardly more than a certain amount of casual information, and even if in some subsequent courses in Dictation a weak attempt is made to fill the gaps left open in the beginning, no real fundamental knowledge can be gained by so defective a method.

This book seeks to provide exercises which—if applied in the right way —must infallibly supply such fundamental theoretical knowledge. It is by no means the first comprehensive attempt to discuss elementary material. It does not even pretend to present this material in an original form. Its content has been set forth and explained countless times before, and there are some excellent books on the subject in various languages. But in order to understand the best works in this field and to make the proper use of them, one must already be a fairly advanced musician. Such a musician will find in them a remarkably good survey of the basic material, but a beginner will hardly be in a position to digest the overwhelming mass and variety of facts and procedures, or to select what is useful for him. Moreover, the exercises given in such books (when any are given) are insufficient.

There is, on the other hand, no lack of less comprehensive, more specialized works, full of exercises for the beginner. But here the difficulty is that those books that try to give general theoretical instruction are either antiquated, in opinion and approach, or insufficient for a professional's education; and in most cases their exercises seem to be made for the author's satisfaction and self-assertion rather than for the student's profit, or they are so dry that even the most docile user cannot see their relationship to living music.

There are numerous highly specialized text-books on Dictation, Sight-Singing and Sight-Reading, Ear-Training, Clef-Reading, and other subdivisions of our subject. But anyone who wished to collect his knowledge by picking it grain by grain out of comparatively elaborate books on comparatively minor subjects would have to spend years on that part of his musical education—which, after all, is but a preparation for more important things to come.

A musician brought up on the method of Solfège, as practised in countries under the influence of French or Italian musical culture, will probably deny that there could be any better method. And if one knows the compritively high standard in sight-reading of melodic and rhythmic patterns (even higher in the rapid pronounciation of the solmisation syllables!) reached by students of this method, one is tempted to agree. But the disadvantages of this method show up later in the musician's course of study: it is extremely difficult to introduce students so trained to a higher conception of harmony and melody, and to bring them to a certain independence in their own creative work. They either cannot take the step out of their narrow concept of tonality (which by the uniform nomenclature for a tone *and* all its derivations is distorted almost to the point where reason turns into nonsense!), or they plunge more easily than others into what is assumed to be a new freedom: tonal disorder and incoherence.

There are still other methods which try to remedy the weakness of Solfège by expressing through all kinds of symbols (in writing, speech, and gesture) the meanings of the scale tones. These range from primitive information for amateurs to most consistently developed "functional" systems. The first category is negligible for the professional musician—unless he wants to specialize in the teaching of amateurs—since it leads him no further than the first steps in the spatial and temporal conception of music. The second category erects in addition to (or instead of) our normal everyday elementary training other systems of theory, the assimilation of which takes more effort and time than the musician not specializing in theory can well afford.

No textbook, whatever the honest intentions of its author, and whatever the quality of its plan and contents, will remain uncriticized. I can easily foresee what the objections to the present book will be.

It will be said that the book is too comprehensive to be used by everyone. The student seeking only some superficial information does not want to digest too many uninteresting things. The highly specialized musician of today, knowing thoroughly the facts and procedures in his particular field of activity, cannot be expected to know everything. Helpful as it may be for a future conductor to have some experience in reading the various clefs, it would be a waste of time for a pianist to bother with such special problems. To sing the right tones at the right time may prove valuable for a singer, but when will a violinist ever be asked to do so? The violinist, in turn, must learn to be fluent in reading high notes, with many ledger lines, while such fluency can be of no value to a timpanist. Essential prerequisites for a player in an orchestra may be utterly unimportant for a virtuoso; increased knowledge of theoretical facts will not instantly improve a cellist's playing; practical experience in music is not necessarily a criterion for the quality of a composer's or theorist's ideas.

There is only one answer to these objections: they are unfounded. The exercises in this book are, in the first place, not written for the amateur's superficial information (although this kind of work will do him no harm, if he is interested). The words "for musicians" in the book's title define clearly its purpose. On the other hand, objections to all-round elementary training for musicians—such as is attempted in this book—can be voiced only by those who acquiesce in the present wide-spread deterioration in musical education.

Apparently the times are gone when no one was considered a good musician who did not possess, beyond his specialized instrumental or vocal achievements, a thorough knowledge of the subtle mechanism of music. Can the majority of to-day's great virtuosi stand a comparison of their theoretical knowledge with Liszt's, Rubinstein's, or Joachim's? Do not many of them bitterly complain that in their youth they were trained excessively in their special craft and not sufficiently in general musical subjects? Theoretical knowledge certainly will not directly improve a violinist's finger-technique; but is it not likely to broaden his musical horizon and influence his ability to interpret a composition? If our performers—players, singers, and conductors alike—had a better insight into the essentials of musical scores, we would not be faced with what seems to have become almost a rule in the superficially over-polished performances of today: either the rattling through of a piece without any reasonable articulation, without any deeper penetration into its character, tempo, expression, meaning, and effect—or the hyper-individualistic distortion of the ideas expressed in a composer's score.

As for singers, nobody denies that most of them are launched on their careers not because they show any extraordinary musical talents, but because they happen to have good voices. On account of this advantage a singer is usually excused from any but the most primitive musical knowledge—knowledge such as could be acquired by any normal mind in a few weeks of intelligent effort. Rare indeed is the singer nowadays who can do what you would expect to be the most normal of all the activities of a singing musician: hit a tone at any interval, even if it is not part of a simple stepwise progression or an easily understandable broken-chord melody, and even if it is not directly supported by its accompaniment. Would a singer not profit by being led through a severe course of general musical training? It certainly would not hurt his voice to gain some additional knowledge, which, although it will not immediately further his vocal aims, amounts after all to no more than that minimum of basic facts that a professional musician is supposed to know.

Admittedly, a composer can have wonderful ideas without a background of highly developed practical experience. But is it really imaginable that without such experience he should be able to present his ideas in their strongest form, and exploit them to the fullest extent? Owing to the general decline of such experience, the composer, once venerated as a super-musician, nowadays occupies almost the lowest ranks of musicianship as far as handicraft is concerned. How few are the composers of today whose achievements are based on their activities as players or singers—in bygone times considered the only sound and stable basis for creative work! All too often we see it happen that a fellow who is not good enough—physically or intellectually—for any instrumental or vocal work still finds a comfortable and uncontested place in the field of composition. The decision to become a composer is in many cases based on no better musical talent than that of listening to records and turning them at the right time (when a mechanical record-changer doesn't eliminate even this last remainder of musical "activity"). Is it strange then, that any tootling, key-pounding, or merely victrola- and radio-active high-school boy who has not written his first symphony before he is through his first year of harmony is already looked on with scorn by his classmates?

I should think that in this situation any method would be welcomed that aimed at keeping our noble guild of composers free of the nitwits and the ungifted. No composer-to-be or future theory teacher who after some practising is not able to do the exercises in the present book easily and thoroughly should be admitted to more advanced theoretical work. In a higher sense he ought to be regarded as unfit for any professional musical activity—which process of reckless weeding out could only be advantageous to our entire musical culture.

For those however, who by their natural musical gift and intelligence are eligible for any of the branches of musical activity, such a method will be the sound basis for their further musical development. They will find in the present book all a musician needs as a preparation for higher theoretical and practical studies, offered without detours and evasions. The book does not use solmisation syllables, since they are misleading. It avoids special names and fancy symbols, since they distract attention from the main object: the knowledge of all the basic conventions and facts of musical theory and their traditional representation in written form. This knowledge is presented through the most intensive kind of work: exercises. The great number of exercises compels the student to practise seriously. Thus it will be demonstrated that Elementary Theory cannot be learned by simply having superficial information handed out for one or two semesters, or without incessant exertion of the student's intellectual capacities. In his very first steps he must be converted from an attentive listener into a working musician. This can be accomplished only by making him articulate. The familiar type of theory class, in which one never hears a tone of music, sung or played, except for the chords pounded out on the piano by the teacher, must disappear! Such classes are as silly as is the usual splitting up of Elementary Training into separate courses of Instruction and Dictation, or of Harmony into "Written" and "Keyboard" courses. It certainly makes more demands upon a teacher to lead a class through an all-round course of theory or harmony, with its constant cross-references to the different sections of the student's activities, than to follow the comfortable, unimaginative path of a split-up course.

A lazy teacher will always present this excuse: How can a beginners' class be articulate if the students can neither sing nor play decently? The answer is that the teacher himself must make them sing and play—not like singers or advanced players, but so that they can open their mouths (willingly!) and produce tones just as any singer in a chorus does. It is quite common to find excellent instrumentalists (not to mention composers) who have gone through six or more years of practical and theoretical studies without ever having opened their mouths for the most natural of all musical utterances! What is true for singing is true for playing, too: every student can strike the keys of the piano enough to play primitive exercises, and if he is not constantly obliged to follow rules of fingering, hand position, and other technical directions, and if we give him time to practise those exercises, he may even develop a kind of unprejudiced, preliminary skill of playing, which can easily be used as a favorable preparation for future regular piano instruction. The same is true for all other instruments, on which, of course, many of the exercises can be played.

After these observations the aim of this book ought to be clear: it is *activity*. Activity for the teacher as well as for the student. Our point of departure is this advice to the teacher: Never teach anything without demonstrating it by writing and singing, or playing; check each exercise by a counter-exercise that uses other means of expression. And for the student: Don't believe any statement unless you see it demonstrated and proved; and don't start writing or singing or playing any exercise before you understand perfectly its theoretical purpose. To produce this kind of compelling activation demands some additional work from the teacher: the *statements* in this book are reduced to their shortest, most condensed form, which in most cases will be too difficult for the average student to understand. Hence the teacher is obliged to dilute and predigest this material, he must find his own way to a more detailed demonstration. The *exercises*, on the other hand, are to be used in the form presented; but, even so, ample opportunity is given for further activities. Frequently enough the teacher will face the necessity of inventing additional exercises, and the student's imagination is constantly spurred by the recurring remark "Invent similar examples." Particularly eager students will find supplementary tests for their wits and their zeal in certain sections of exercises, marked "More difficult."

Each chapter of the book is divided into three sections, *A. Action in Time; B. Action in Space; C. Coordinated Action.* The first section contains exercises in Rhythm and Meter, both in their basic forms. Theories and exercises pertaining to the higher aspect of Rhythm—Musical Form—do not belong in this context of elementary training, but have their place in the curriculum of the advanced student, where they may be taught by the deductive method of Form Analysis, or the inductive method of Composition. (For similar reasons, no historical facts are given.) Action in Space comprises instruction about pitch, intervals, and scales, which in Coordinated Action is combined with the rhythmic and metric experiences of the first section. No information on chords, harmonic progression, or melodic structure is included, since this is likewise a part of more advanced theory courses. Interspersed in all three sections are complete courses in Notation and Dictation. Exercises for the latter, however, are given in the second part of the book, which during instruction in class is to be used by the teacher only, in order to preserve for the student the factor of unfamiliarity, essential to any kind of dictation.

The first two chapters contain exercises which without any effort can be done even by the most ungifted pupil. But from there on the material given can be mastered only by consistent practising, done in class and as homework. Even a talented student will notice that in order to overcome the progressively mounting difficulties he cannot depend on his musical instinct alone, but will be compelled to develop his ability to think logically, his acuteness, and his capacity for combining various elements. If teacher and student attack this task in the right spirit, as a well-coordinated team, the book's material will keep them busy for a year and a half or two years.

The question may arise how this material can be incorporated in a normal student's curriculum. My opinion is that nobody should be admitted to a harmony class unless he is able to do the exercises in at least the first two thirds of this book. The advantages are obvious: a student thoroughly trained in the basic principles of music is undoubtedly better prepared than other students for the understanding of harmonic technique and for rapid progress in mastering it. Such well-prepared students will not need other auxiliary courses (such as dictation and other *pontes asinorum*).

The book grew out of the demands of my classes in theory, and was written for the benefit of my students. Needless to say, then: all the examples have been tested thoroughly, and only those have been included that have proved their usefulness—this as an answer to the fears of the doubtful and the short-sighted.

New Haven, Conn.   PAUL HINDEMITH
Yale University
Spring. 1946

Part One

STATEMENTS AND EXERCISES

CHAPTER I

A. Action in Time

The most primitive form of temporal action in music is the use of tones of different length.

—— EXERCISE 1 ——

1. Tap with a pencil, or clap with your hands, or tap (standing in place or walking) with your feet, in moderate tempo a series of rhythmic strokes, at equal intervals of time:

| | | | | | | | | | | | | | | | | | | etc.

2. While tapping (or clapping), sing one long tone without changing its pitch:

tone: ‾‾‾‾‾‾‾‾‾‾‾‾‾‾‾‾‾‾‾‾‾‾‾‾‾‾‾‾‾‾‾‾‾
rhythm: | | | | | | | | | | | | | | | | | | | | | | | | etc.

3. Tap or clap the rhythm as before but sing the tone only on the strokes connected by brackets. All singing throughout this book is to be done on la la, unless other instructions are given.

(a)
(b)
(c)
(d)
(e)
(f)
(g)
(h)

Invent similar examples.

5. Instead of singing the tone, play it on an instrument and tap the rhythm with one foot. If you use the piano:

    (a) Play each exercise with the right hand and tap the rhythm;
    (b) Play with the left hand; tap;
    (c) Play with the right hand; tap the thythm with the left hand;
    (d) Play with the left hand; tap with the right hand.
    You will notice that there is a remarkable difference in difficulty between (c) and (d), and in similar cases throughout the book. Try each of these reversed-hands examples in very slow tempo at first, increasing the speed with each playing. More than any other exercises these will prove a touchstone for your independence of physical action and mental coordination.

6. Do all these examples in an accelerated tempo.

—— *DICTATION 1*

NOTATION: The rhythms and the different lengths of tones in the preceding exercises can be represented by notes:

    O = *whole-note;* corresponds with the tones whose duration was four claps or taps (metric beats),

    ♩ or ♩ = *half-note;* duration of two beats: ⌐⌐ The dash is called a *stem.* Up-stems are attached to the right side of the note-head, down-stems to the left.

    ♩ or ♩ = *quarter-note;* one beat |

—— EXERCISE 2 ——

1. Sing and tap as before:

[4]

(c)

(d)

(e)

—— *DICTATION 2*

Notation: (1) The omission of tones or rhythms is indicated by *rests*:

= silence equalling ○

= 𝅗𝅥

= ♩

(2) The ending of each example is marked by a *double bar*: ‖

—— EXERCISE 3 ——

1. Play and tap as before:

(a)

(b)

(c)

(d)

(e)

[5]

2. Invent, sing, and play similar examples.

—— *DICTATION 3*

B. Action in Space

The most primitive form of "spatial" action in music is expressed by singing or playing tones of different *pitch*.

—— EXERCISE 4 ——

1. Sing one steady tone of a few seconds' duration at a pitch comfortable for your voice; then sing a tone of a somewhat higher pitch; go back to the first tone; sing a tone somewhat lower; go back to the first tone.

2. The three tones may be marked m (middle), h (high), l (low). Now sing the following exercises:

   (a) m m h m

   (b) m l m l m

   (c) m h m m l m

   (d) m l·l m h h m

   (e) h m l m h m

   (f) l m l m h m l m h m

   (g) h l m l h m h l m

   (h) l h h l l h m

[6]

3. Invent similar exercises.

C. Coordinated Action

Our three symbols of note-values (𝐨, 𝅗𝅥, ♩) may be placed upon, above, or below a line, marking the position of the middle, high, or low tone.

NOTATION: The rest equivalent to 𝐨 (whole-rest) is written hanging down from the line; the half-rest sticks up from the line; the quarter-rest can be placed above, on, or below the line.

—— EXERCISE 5 ——

1. Sing the notes; tap the beats:

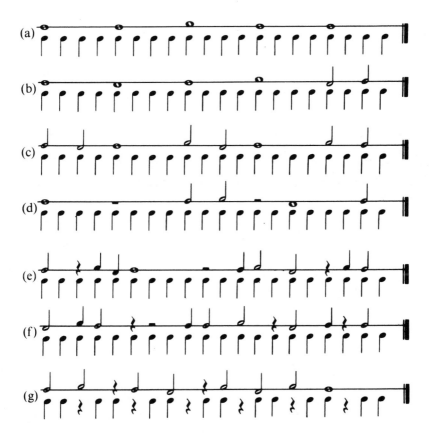

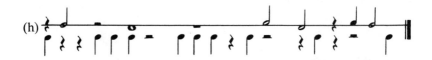

(h)

2. Play the upper notes in the preceding exercises, tapping the lower ones. (On the piano, play with one hand and tap with the other; then change.)

3. Invent similar exercises.

—— *DICTATION 4*

CHAPTER II

A. Action in Time

The rhythmic values of $\mathbf{o}$, $\downarrow$ and $\downarrow$, and the equivalent rests may be organized in regular groups of two or four beats.

NOTATION: (1) Such groups are divided by *bar-lines:* | | | The space between two bar-lines is called a *measure.*

(2) The constant number of beats between two bar-lines is indicated at the beginning of each example by the numerator of a common fraction (*time-signature*). The denominator shows what unit is to be counted as one beat ($\downarrow$ = $\frac{1}{4}\mathbf{o}$): $\frac{2}{4}$, $\frac{4}{4}$. $\frac{4}{4}$-time may also be marked $\mathbf{C}$

(3) The rest for a complete measure is always ▬ , whatever the time-signature may be, and it is always placed in the middle of the measure.

A note filling a complete measure is also placed in the middle of the measure except when shorter notes are written above or below it, to be sounded simultaneously with it. In such cases the long note is placed at the beginning of the measure.

—— EXERCISE 6 ——

1. Play (any tone) and tap. (In playing the piano follow the instructions given in Ex. 1, par. 5, p. 4.)

(d)

2. Invent similar examples, write them down, and play them.

3. Play and count aloud (instead of tapping):

4. Invent similar examples, write them down, and play them.

—— *DICTATION 5*

5. Sing. Instead of counting aloud, count mentally.

6. Invent similar examples.

—— *DICTATION 6*

B. Action in Space

The middle, high, and low tones used in the preceding chapter are now to be used as tones of fixed pitch, having a fixed pitch-relationship to one another.

The middle tone is the tone *a*, which is to be found by using a tuning fork that produces this tone. In examples to be sung, women's and children's voices sing this tone; men's voices sing the tone *a* in the register comfortable for them (one octave lower).

NOTATION: (1) The one line used before is insufficient for higher purposes. We replace it by the *staff*, consisting of 5 lines:

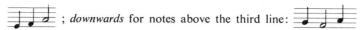 with four spaces:

(2) The tones are represented by the note-values (𝅝 𝅗𝅥 𝅘𝅥) placed upon the lines or in the spaces:

(3) The stems of notes are drawn *upwards* for notes below the third line:

; *downwards* for notes above the third line:

The stems of notes on the third line may be drawn in either direction, but are more often drawn downwards.

(4) The name and meaning of the notes are determined by *clefs*.

The *g-* or *treble* clef: 𝄞 winds around the second line: , the

note on this line being called *g*:

(5) This tone *g* is the lower neighbor of the tone *a*, produced by the tuning

fork: The highest of our three tones is *b:*

In examples to be sung, the procedure is always as follows:

(a) strike the tuning fork;
(b) taking its tone, *a*, as a starting-point, try to hear in your imagination the first tone of the example;
(c) sing this tone first; then the other tones of the example.

1. Sing:

NOTATION: A *hold* or *fermata* 𝄐 over a note or a rest shows that the regular counting of rhythmic beats is suspended and the tone or pause is of indefinite length—in most cases longer than the value indicated by the note or rest.

2. Sing: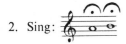

Check the *b* on the piano. (Is it necessary to mention that the piano *a* and the tone of the fork must be identical in pitch?)

3. Sing:

Check the *g* on the piano.

4. Sing:

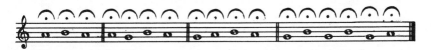

NOTATION: Sectional endings of a piece are marked: ‖

The distance *a-b* and *g-a* is called a *whole-tone* (don't confuse with the whole-*note!*).

—— EXERCISE 8 ——

1. Try to sing one whole-tone lower than *g*. Check on the piano.

NOTATION: This tone is called *f* and is written:

[13]

2. Sing:

—— *DICTATION 7*

C. Coordinated Action

—— EXERCISE 9 ——

1. Sing, clapping or tapping:

(*Whenever you find two lines of notes in this book, the lower one, not written on a staff, is to be tapped or clapped.*)

2. Play (as in Ex. 1, par. 5, p. 4):

DICTATION 8

NOTATION: A rest for the two middle quarters of a $\frac{4}{4}$ measure is written:

3. Sing rather fast, counting mentally:

la la la la la etc.

CHAPTER III

A. Action in Time

In the preceding exercises the unit of a rhythmic beat was indicated by $\quarternote$, the quarter-note. The two other note-values counted two beats ($\halfnote$) and four beats ($\wholenote$) respectively. Instead of multiplying the quarter-note, we can divide it into *eighth*-notes or *sixteenth*-notes.

NOTATION: (1) Single eighth-notes are written like quarters, but with a *flag* or *hook* added to the stem: $\eighthnote\eighthnote$. The flag is always attached to the right-hand side, regardless of the upward or downward direction of the stem.

Single sixteenth-notes have two flags: $\sixteenthnote\sixteenthnote$. The corresponding rests are $\eighthrest$ and $\sixteenthrest$ *

(2) Two or more $\eighthnote$ or $\sixteenthnote$ may be connected by a *beam:*

also in combinations:

(3) The beams of eighth-notes mark either the quarters or the halves of a measure:

Less desirable:

Not:

*The eighth-rest $\eighthrest$ is easily confused with $\quarterrest$ which in some French, Italian, and English editions is used as a quarter-rest.

The beams of sixteenth-notes mark the eighths or quarters:

Less desirable:

In $\frac{4}{4}$ time they do not connect the second and third quarters. Not:

For combined beams the quarter is generally used as the unit in $\frac{4}{4}$ and $\frac{4}{4}$:

Less frequently:

(4) The distribution of the beams in $\frac{4}{4}$ follows the rule that the two halves of a $\frac{4}{4}$ measure must be recognizable. In measures where no beams occur it is not always possible to maintain this division strictly. Sometimes it can be maintained only in less perfect form when one note (♩ or ♪) is placed in the middle of the measure, so that one half of its value belongs to the second beat and the other to the third:

But the following, which completely contradicts this rule, is very unclear:

The notation of such complex rhythmic patterns will be explained in Chapter IV.

(5) Direction of stems in groups connected by beams: upwards or downwards according to the general statement on page 12 (Notation, par. 3). In groups of notes some of which would require upward and some downward stems, all stems are drawn in the same direction, which is that required by the note farthest from the middle line:

In doubtful cases, downward stems are generally preferable:

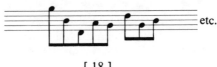

[18]

Question: What is the number of

(a) eighths in ♩ ♩ ......, in 𝅝 ......?

(b) sixteenths in ♩ ......, in 𝅝 ......?

—— EXERCISE 10 ——

1. Sing:

More difficult:

NOTATION: A rest for the two middle eighths in $\frac{2}{4}$ time or in one of the halves of a $\frac{4}{4}$ measure is written ,

not

2. Play:

(a)

(b)

(c)

(d)

More difficult:

(e)

(f)

(g)

—— DICTATION 10

3. Sing, counting mentally:

(a)

(b)

(c)

(6) Sometimes the beams are written bridging over a bar line. This is to be regarded as abnormal, however, and should be applied only when a complicated rhythmic distribution of notes would gain in legibility by this kind of notation.

More difficult:

—— DICTATION 11

B. Action in Space

To our four tones *f g a b* we add one higher tone (*c*) and one lower (*e*). The distance between each of these two tones and its neighbor (*c-b* and *e-f*) is, unlike that between any other two adjacent tones used hitherto, not a whole-tone, but a *half*-tone.

—— EXERCISE 11 ——

1. Try to sing: *a* (use the fork) *b c;* check the *c* on the piano; *a g f e;* check the *e*.

[23]

NOTATION:

In notation there is no distinction between whole-tone and half-tone steps. Compare the notation of the whole-tone step *g-a* with that of the half-tone

b-c: 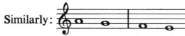 (in both cases: a line and the next higher

space).

Similarly:

2. Sing with a hold or fermata on each tone:

—— *DICTATION 12*

C. Coordinated Action

—— **EXERCISE 12** ——

1. Sing:

More difficult:

2. Play (see remark 5 on page 4):

More difficult:

—— DICTATION 13

3. Play, counting the beats aloud. (Don't sing.)

In order to facilitate the counting of complicated rhythmic patterns, one may count each beat with two syllables, thus:

one-and, two-and, etc.

1   and   2   and   1   and   2   and   etc.

More difficult:

4. Sing, counting mentally:

(a)

(b)

More difficult:

(c)

(d)

[29]

CHAPTER IV

A. Action in Time

We use tones with a duration of three beats.

NOTATION: (1) There is no independent rhythmic symbol for such a tone. We write it with the next smaller (two-beat) value and add a dot. The dot adds to the note one half of its rhythmic value (*augmentation dot*):

𝅗𝅥. = 𝅗𝅥 + 𝅘𝅥 ; consequently: one 𝅗𝅥. contains ...... 𝅘𝅥𝅮 , and ...... 𝅘𝅥𝅯 (fill in).

(2) The dotted half-note (𝅗𝅥.) may fill an entire measure; the time-signature for such a measure is $\frac{3}{4}$. Or it is put into the context of $\frac{4}{4}$ or $\frac{2}{4}$ measures. It may be so placed that its duration is divided by the bar line into unequal parts, in $\frac{3}{4}$ as well as in $\frac{2}{4}$ or $\frac{4}{4}$. In such cases the augmentation dot is replaced by a *tie*:

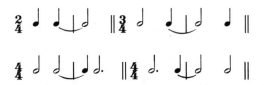

$\frac{2}{4}$, $\frac{3}{4}$, and $\frac{4}{4}$ are called *simple meter*.

A dotted half-note cannot be used as the middle note in a $\frac{4}{4}$ measure so that $\frac{3}{8}$ of its value are a part of the first half of the measure, and the other $\frac{3}{8}$ of the second. (See p. 18, Notation 4.) Not  When this rhythmic figure occurs it can only be written with tied notes which show clearly the distribution of note-values in a $\frac{4}{4}$ measure as mentioned before:

$\frac{4}{4}$ 𝅘𝅥𝅘𝅥𝅗𝅥 𝅘𝅥𝅘𝅥 |

(3) The tie is also used when any other note-value extends from one measure into the next, divided by the bar-line into either equal or unequal parts:

(4) Augmentation dots are not used in combination with half-rests, in simple meter.* The equivalent of ♩. in ⁴₄ is ▬ ‚ , or ‚ ▬ , always so placed that the two halves of the measure are recognizable. Thus:

⁴₄ ♩ ‚ ▬ | ▬ ‚ ♩ ‖ but not: ⁴₄ ♩ ▬ ‚ ‖

In ³₄ the ▬ is not used, a rest of two beats always being written ‚ ‚ , and a rest of three beats being written ▬ since it fills a whole measure.

(5) The beams of eighth-notes in ³₄ time mark the rhythmic unity either of the whole measure(♫♫♫), or of the quarters and halves

(♫ ♫ ♫ | ♫ ♫♫ | ♫♫ ♫) etc., but not:

*Cf. p. 106.

[31]

etc. Beams of sixteenth-notes mark the eighths or quarters:

etc. Less desirable:

etc.

—— EXERCISE 13 ——

1.Sing:

(a)

(b)

(c)

More difficult:

2. Play:

(c) 2/4

 DICTATION 14

NOTATION: Ties are used not only to connect the values of notes before and after a bar-line, but also to connect notes within the same measure when the metric divisions of the measure would not be clear with other notation:

More difficult:

(d) 2/4

(e) 3/4

[34]

3. Sing, counting mentally:

(a)

(b)

(c)

More difficult:

—— DICTATION 15

B. Action in Space

We add two more tones below the *e:* the *d* and the *c.*

NOTATION: The *d* is written below the lines:

For the *c* we use a *ledger line:*

Thus our tones have a range from the so-called *middle c* to its higher repetition. This space is called an *octave.* In order to distinguish this octave from other octaves it is called the *one-lined,* octave. It contains the *one-lined c,* the *one-lined d,* and so forth to the *one-lined b.* The higher *c* is the *two-lined c,* the first tone of the *two-lined octave.*

Reason for this nomenclature: In cases where the tones have to be symbolized by letters of the alphabet instead of notes (theory exercises, scientific treatises, etc.) the different octaves are distinguished by small lines added to the letters representing tones. Hence tones used so far have the following symbols:

c′ d′ e′ f′ g′ a′ b′ c″

[36]

1. Sing tones with holds:

Check the *d* and *c* on the piano.

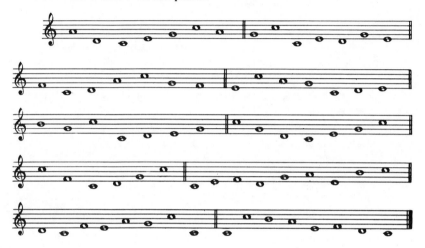

2. Invent similar examples.

—— *DICTATION 16*

NOTATION: (1) A *slur*, connecting two or more notes of different pitch (*Question:* What does a tie do?) indicates that the tones represented by these notes are to be produced without interruption or individual articulation. The effect of slurring is especially obvious in singing, where the slur demands that a single syllable extend over all the slurred tones, instead of the more usual procedure in singing: one syllable to each tone.

(2) In writing text to slurred notes, a horizontal line after a monosyllabic word, or the last syllable of a polysyllabic word, marks the coincidence of word and slur:

ear _____

[37]

while division of words is shown by repeated hyphens:

fin – – – – ger

(3) Unslurred eighths and sixteenths with separate text-syllables are written with flags instead of beams:

la la la la not la la la la

This rule is not observed very consistently, however, especially when a great number of flagged notes would result in a definitely lower degree of legibility than notation with beams. But in the notation of the melodies to be sung we shall adhere from now on strictly to the rule.

(4) In groups of notes connected by one beam it is not necessary to indicate an extended syllable by slurs. Thus:

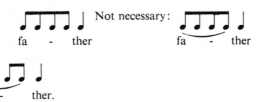

fa - ther   Not necessary: fa - ther

But:

fa - ther.

(5) Notes with stems are slurred preferably at the heads of the notes, not at the stem-ends:

, not

For groups with stems in both directions, there is no hard and fast rule:

or , or

Less desirable:

(6) Slurs starting or ending with tied notes can be written in either of two ways:

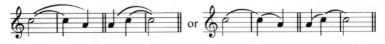

or

A tie included in a slur is unaffected by it:

(7) In instrumental music slurs serve several different purposes. As symbols of *articulation* they tell the player of

wind instruments: "play the slurred notes without interruption."

stringed instruments: "play them with a single stroke of the bow."

keyboard instruments: "don't interrupt by lifting the fingers from the keys between the tones; play as 'legato' (evenly sustained, connected) as possible."

As symbols of *phrasing* (especially in keyboard music) they indicate the sections of melodic lines of some length.

C. Coordinated Action

—— EXERCISE 15 ——

1. Sing:

More difficult:

—— *DICTATION 17*

2. Play:

More difficult:

—— *DICTATION 18*

Pieces need not begin on the first beat. Instead, they may begin on any fractional part of the measure.

NOTATION: The full measure, however, has to be written out (beginning with one or more rests) when the sounding fractional part is more than one half measure in $\frac{2}{4}$ or $\frac{4}{4}$, and more than two quarters in $\frac{3}{4}$. In all other cases—i.e., one half measure or less in $\frac{2}{4}$ and $\frac{4}{4}$; two quarters or less in $\frac{3}{4}$ (*up-beats*)—no rests are written. In shorter pieces the "up-beat" and the ending measure complement one another to make one full measure.

1. Play, and count aloud (don't sing):

More difficult:

2. Sing, counting mentally. (These and similar exercises are easier to sing if certain important tones are accented. Wherever two or more notes are tied, any accent should be applied only to the first, except where otherwise expressly indicated.)

NOTATION: An accent is written > (in some editions ∧).

More difficult:

la _____ la ___ la   etc.

la la _____   la la ____   la la   etc.

—— DICTATION 19

CHAPTER V

A. Action in Time

NOTATION: Besides the note-values of $\frac{3}{8}$ and $\frac{3}{16}$, caused by tieing-over quarter-, eighth-, and sixteenth-notes, as discussed in the preceding chapter, other (untied) $\frac{3}{8}$ and $\frac{3}{16}$ values are obtained by adding the augmentation dot to the quarter- and eighth-note respectively.

[music notation example]

A ♩. with additional note- or rest-values can be used in $\frac{2}{4}$, $\frac{3}{4}$, and $\frac{4}{4}$ time whenever a half-note would be possible.

[music notation examples]

Less desirable:

[music notation example]

Frequently used:

[music notation example]   although the beats of the $\frac{3}{4}$ meter are not shown clearly.

Poor legibility, which in certain cases may result from using the ♪. , can be avoided by applying the tie instead of the dot:

[music notation example] , instead of [music notation example]

[music notation example] , instead of [music notation example]

The rest having the value of $\frac{3}{8}$ is [rest symbol] . In simple meter it is never used except as the beginning of a $\frac{2}{4}$ or $\frac{4}{4}$ measure, or as the beginning of the second half of a $\frac{4}{4}$ measure:

[music notation example]

In all other cases the combination ⁊ [rest] or [rest] ⁊ is used.

[45]

The ♪. is used similarly to the ♩. , namely with an additional ♪ or 𝄾 making up the value of a quarter note. This rule, however, is not followed too strictly, and frequently—legibility permitting—one finds a ♪. in groups that add up to the value of a ♩ , especially when the ♪. is part of a group united by beams (the beams in such cases being applied according to the rules given on p. 17.)

etc.

etc.

etc.

Not recommended: etc.

etc.

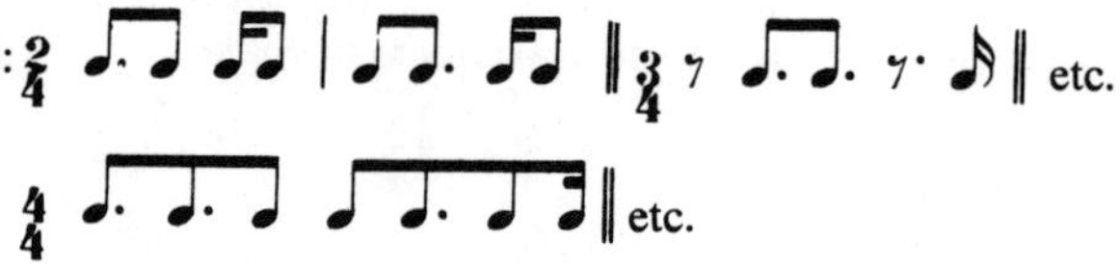

The $\frac{3}{16}$ rest (𝄾·) serves exclusively as the beginning or ending of a quarter unit.

Not:

etc.

—— EXERCISE 17 ——

1. Sing. In exercises to be sung, mark with a ' the points where you breathe, and in repeated singing of an exercise always breathe at the same place.

(a)

(b)

More difficult:

(c) [musical notation]

(d) [musical notation]

2. Play:

(a) [musical notation]

(b)

More difficult:

(c)

(d)

3. Play, counting the beats aloud:

(a)

More difficult:

NOTATION: (1) If the regular number of beats in the measures of a piece changes, a change of time-signature has to be marked after the bar-line. In case the change occurs after the final measure of a staff, the new time-signature has to be marked both after the last bar-line on the old staff, and at the beginning of the new staff.

(2) The *repetition sign* ⫸ implies that a piece or section is to be repeated. If the repetition goes back to the beginning of a piece, no additional sign is necessary. But for repetitions of middle sections the start of the section to be repeated has to be marked thus: ⫷

The repetition sign may take the place of a bar-line but does not necessarily count as one. Consequently a measure may be interrupted by it and continue after it.

4. Sing, count mentally:

More difficult:

B. Action in Space

We complete our series of tones approximately to the extreme range of women's voices (Alto and Soprano) by adding to the octave *c'—c"* lower and higher octave-transpositions of some of its tones.

This creates below the *c'* lower transpositions of *b'*, *a'*, *g'*, *f'*, and *e'*, and above the *c"* higher transpositions of *d'*, *e'*, *f'*, *g'*, *a'*, *b'*, and *c"*.

The tones below *c'* belong to the *small octave* (its tones are represented by the small letters of the alphabet with no line added): *b, a, g, f, e*. The tones above *c"* are: *d"*, *e"*, *f"*, *g"*, *a"*, *b"*, and *c'''*, with which tone the *three-lined octave* begins.

NOTATION: These tones are written:

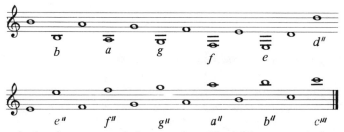

The *e* is already an extremely low note in treble clef (more practical notations exist in other clefs), but the notation of tones with more ledger-lines than *c'''* cannot be avoided, since the *g* clef is the highest clef used.

—— EXERCISE 18 ——

1. Name the following notes (include the name of the octave!):

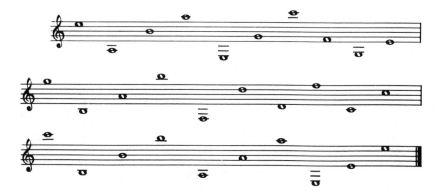

2. Play them on the piano.
3. Play on the piano at random any tones on the white keys within the range *e*—*c'''*, and name them.

—— *DICTATION 21*

The seven tones of the octave *c'*—*b'*, corresponding to one section of the piano consisting of seven white keys in succession, constitute a *major scale*.

In order to show the structure of a major scale, the higher octave of the first tone is usually added after the seventh tone.

A major scale is a succession of whole-tone and half-tone steps, the order of which is invariably the same as in the scale on *c'*:

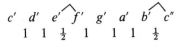

$$c' \quad d' \quad e' \quad f' \quad g' \quad a' \quad b' \quad c''$$
$$1 \quad 1 \quad \tfrac{1}{2} \quad 1 \quad 1 \quad 1 \quad \tfrac{1}{2}$$

Major scales may be constructed on any tone. These scales always follow strictly the principle of construction described, which causes the half-tone steps to occur between different pairs of tones in each scale. Now since, on the other hand, in our seven basic tones the half-tone steps invariably lie between *e*—*f* and *b*—*c*, we must obviously find new tones in order to make possible the construction of scales on other tones than *c*.

The seven unrepeated tones from *c* to *b* are our complete basic material. Therefore the new tones needed can be obtained only by derivation from these seven basic tones.

For the construction of a major scale on *g* we find the half-tone step between the third and fourth tones already provided among the seven basic tones (*b*—*c*), but not the one between the seventh and eighth. Therefore the seventh tone (*f*) has to be raised one half-tone.*

*In the tuning of our modern keyboard instruments the half-tone is (at least theoretically) one half of the whole-tone, and in the disposition of the keyboard, which shows each black key placed between two whites, we recognize this fact easily. But in non-keyboard instruments and in human voices the half-tone is by no means necessarily half of a whole-tone. Moreover, the whole-tone itself does not have in its natural form the size it has in the so-called equally tempered tuning of the piano—in fact it appears in at least two different sizes. For our immediate purposes these highly theoretical distinctions can be disregarded, and it suffices to regard the half-tone as actually one half of the (standardized) whole-tone.

NOTATION: (1) The raising of a tone is indicated by a *sharp* (♯), placed before the head of a note. Raised tones are called by their original names, with the word *sharp* added:

("one-lined *g* sharp," "two-lined *d* sharp")

(2) In notation (but not on the keyboard!) there are two different types of half-tone steps. One is called the *diatonic half-tone*. Its two tones, though one of them or even both may be derivations (♯ added), belong to two different basic tones and are written on different degrees of the staff:

Note that on the keyboard *e* sharp = *f*, and *b* sharp = *c*.
The two tones of the *chromatic half-tone* belong to a single basic tone, one is derived from the other:

The sign ♮ (*natural*) shows that after a sharp (♯) the original basic tone is to be restored.

(3) Obviously there are different ways of writing certain tone combinations, as the diatonic and chromatic forms of the following half-step show:

In complicated harmonic situations it is in fact sometimes difficult to decide which notation is the correct one. But in constructing major scales no doubts will ever arise. The half-tone steps in the model scale on *c* are diatonic, not chromatic; accordingly the other scales, as copies of this model, can never contain any chromaticism.

—— EXERCISE 19 ——

Construct major scales on

upwards through one octave.

First write them down. Then read and sing them, pronouncing the name of each tone. Then—without using the written example—play them on the piano, again pronouncing the names.

NOTATION: The letters of the alphabet representing the names of major scales are always written as capitals.

Question: What is the number of sharps needed for each scale:

G......, D......, A......, E......, B......?

Pieces that use the tones of the C major scale are called *in C major,* or *in the key* (or *tonality*) *of C major.* Similarly, we can speak of pieces in G major, B major, etc.

NOTATION: The sharps necessary for the construction of major scales—or, what is the same, for the expression of a tonality*—can be put at the beginning of each staff line. They then raise all the notes of the same letter-name in the staff, not only in their own octave but in all other octaves as well. Thus the ♯ put on the top line raises all *f*'s:

Question: Can you name the tonalities represented by the following groups of accidentals (*key-signatures*)?

N.B. These are standard patterns. The accidentals for A major, for instance, should never be written:

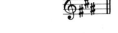

C. Coordinated Action

—— EXERCISE 20 ——

1. Sing major scales through one octave upwards, then downwards, following a given rhythmic pattern. Do this several times in succession. Mark the beats (regular quarters). Example:

If the scale on *c* is sung with the rhythmic pattern:

*In more advanced musical contexts the scales and the symbols for altering tones chromatically (*accidentals*) are not the only means of tonal determination!

the effect will be:

Sing on "la," except on tones with a circle. Sing these with their names.

in D major

in B major

in G major

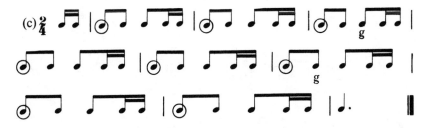

in E major

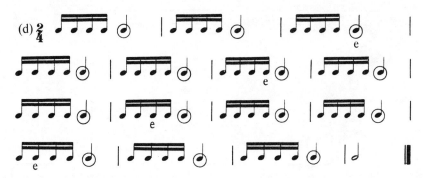

in A major

2. Sing:

More difficult:

[57]

In diatonic scales (diatonic = consisting of whole- and half-tone steps), certain tones have special names.

In our major scale the first tone (or first *degree*) is called the *Tonic;* the fourth: *Subdominant;* the fifth: *Dominant;* the seventh: *Leading Tone.*

Before playing the next exercise, mark in each example all tonics, subdominants, dominants, and leading tones with appropriate symbols (T, S, D, L).

—— EXERCISE 21 ——

1. Play on the piano (using either one or both hands, as convenient) counting aloud:

2. The following melodies are written without key-signature. Sing them, raising the appropriate tones according to the tonalities marked at the beginning of each example:

in A major

(e)

—— *DICTATION 22*

CHAPTER VI

A. Action in Time

Instead of using the quarter-note as the metric unit, we may replace it by any other note-value.

Theoretically we thus obtain the following measures: $\frac{2}{1}$ ($_1$ being the whole-note!), $\frac{3}{1}$, $\frac{4}{1}$; $\frac{2}{2}$ (also written $\mathbf{\phi}$, and called *Alla breve*), $\frac{3}{2}$, $\frac{4}{2}$; $\frac{2}{8}$, $\frac{3}{8}$, $\frac{4}{8}$; $\frac{2}{16}$, $\frac{3}{16}$, $\frac{4}{16}$. But the measurements with the value of the whole-note as denominator, although frequently used in old music, have almost no practical significance today. Neither have the short measures: $\frac{2}{8}$, $\frac{2}{16}$, $\frac{3}{16}$, $\frac{4}{16}$.

Beams in meters with the denominators 8 or 16 either comprise the whole measure or show the beat units.

In $\frac{2}{2}$, $\frac{3}{2}$, and $\frac{4}{2}$, the dotted quarter rest ($\mathbf{\xi}$·) may be written at the beginning of any beat.

The tempo at which the single units of measurement follow each other can be indicated by two different means:

(a) We determine the number of beats in a minute. The instrument that enables us to divide a minute into any given number of beats between about 30 and 200 is the *Metronome*, a pendulum with or without clockwork, or a watchlike or electrical device.

NOTATION: This measurement is indicated above the staff line by: $\mathbf{o} = 60$, $\mathbf{\rfloor} = 84$, $\mathbf{\rfloor} = 108$, $\mathbf{\rfloor} = 134$, $\mathbf{\rfloor} = 164$, etc.; in older editions: M.M.

$\mathbf{o} = 60$, etc. (M.M. meaning Maelzel's Metronome).

(b) We explain by adjectives, participles, or other parts of speech the approximate speed and character of a piece. It is advisable to use English terms for this purpose. The musician, however, is used to the traditional Italian words, or in German and French editions to the terms of those languages.

In this book we omit the first kind of tempo indication, since the speed of our exercises depends mainly on the individual student's skill and ability.

NOTATION: (1) For slow and moderate tempi the following terms are used (Italian, German, and French forms):

Adagio—Langsam, getragen—Lent = slow;

Largo—Breit—Large = broad;

Lento—Langsam—Lent = slow;

[62]

Grave—Schwer—Lourd = heavy;

Andante—Gehend—Allant = (walking), quiet;

Moderato—Mässig, gemässigt—Modéré = moderate.

(2) The meaning of these terms can be intensified or reduced by adding:

(a) *molto* (or *assai*)—*sehr*—*très* = very
    (*molto adagio*—*sehr langsam*—*très lent*);

(b) [*un*] *poco*—*ein wenig, etwas*—*un peu* = somewhat
    (*poco adagio*—*ein wenig langsam*—*un peu lent*).

These are only a few of the most frequently used of a great number of possible suggestive terms.

—— EXERCISE 22 ——

1. Play, counting aloud:

Moderato

Adagio

[63]

[64]

NOTATION: (1) ⊨ (*brevis*) is the note that fills a whole measure in $\frac{4}{2}$ or $\frac{2}{1}$ time.

(2) In $\frac{3}{2}$ and $\frac{4}{2}$ we sometimes encounter the dotted whole note (**o·**), which, like the other dotted notes, is equal to $1\frac{1}{2}$ times its original undotted value:

o· = **o** ♩ or ♩＿♩＿♩ ; accordingly, it contains: . . . . . ♩ ,

. . . . . ♪, ... ♪ (fill in).

2. Sing, counting mentally:

Largo

Lento

Moderato

3. Invent similar examples.

—— *DICTATION 23*

B. Action in Space

Tones higher than *c'''*

NOTATION: (1) The *three-lined octave* is written:

(2) In order to facilitate the reading of notes with many ledger lines, the higher tones of this octave and the following *four-lined octave* may be symbolized by the notes of the next lower octave with the *octave sign* added.

etc.

(3) Sometimes you will find the letter-symbols of the one- to four-lined octaves written thus:

$$c^1 \ldots c^2 \ldots c^3 \ldots c^4 \ldots, \text{ instead of}$$
$$c' \ldots c'' \ldots c''' \ldots c'''' \ldots.$$

—— EXERCISE 23 ——

1. Name (the tones and their octaves) and play on the piano:

2. Play at random on the piano tones higher than *c'''*, and name them.

—— *DICTATION 24*

The seven basic tones can be not only raised (♯) but also lowered.

[66]

NOTATION: (1) The symbol for lowering a tone by one half-tone step is a *flat:* ♭

g' flat d" flat

(2) Diatonic half-tone steps obtained by using flats:

etc.

Chromatic half-tones:

etc.

—— EXERCISE 24 ——

Construct the major scale on *f:*

Write it down, read the names of the tones aloud.

Sing it (through one octave), pronouncing the names. Play it on the piano (through three octaves).

Major scales can be constructed not only on the seven basic tones, but on the raised and lowered tones as well.

—— EXERCISE 25 ——

1. Construct major scales on

Read, sing, and play them according to the instructions in the preceding exercise.

[67]

2. What is the kind and number of accidentals (♯ or ♭) needed to construct the following major scales?

A, B, G, F♯, D♭, D, E, G♭, F, A, E♭, B♭

3. Which tonalities are indicated by the following key-signatures?

C. Coordinated Action
—— EXERCISE 26 ——

1. Sing major scales. Use the rhythmic patterns given in Exercise 20 and follow strictly the instructions given there.

F, B♭, E♭, A♭, D♭, G♭, F♯

2. Sing:

(c) Fast

More difficult:

(e) Poco Andante

(f) Rather fast

[69]

NOTATION: The symbols ⌐1.⌐ ⌐2.⌐ in combination with a repetition sign mean the first ending is to be played before the repetition, the second ending after.

—— *DICTATION 25*

NOTATION: Any accidental (♯, ♭), placed before a note, keeps its validity throughout a measure, but only in its own octave. Thus:

sounds thus:

Accidentals before notes tied over a bar-line are valid till the end of the tie (but the same is *not* true for slurs):

In cases where doubts may arise, an additional though theoretically superfluous ♯ or ♭ will do no harm.

—— EXERCISE 27 ——

1. Play on the piano, counting aloud. The key-signature is not given, but by observing the accidentals of each example you can determine the key.

Moderato

NOTATION: (1) *D.C.* (*Da capo* = "from the head") *al fine* means: Go back to the beginning and proceed to the word *fine* (end), where the piece (or a part of it) ends.

(2) *D.S. al fine*, or *Dal Segno al fine* means that one goes back not to the beginning of the piece but to a place marked by a special sign (*segno*): ⌥ or 𝄋

[71]

2. Sing, adding the accidentals necessary to produce the key marked at the beginning of each example.

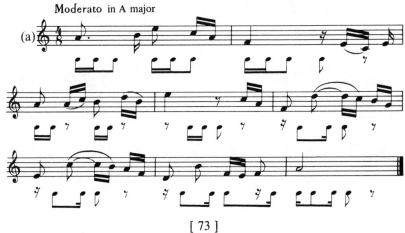

Gay in F♯ major

(b)

Andante in E♭ major

(c)

Rather fast in F major

(d)

More difficult:

Not too fast in B♭ major

(e)

[75]

CHAPTER VII

A. Action in Time

NOTATION: The augmentation dot can be followed by a second dot. As we know, the first dot adds to the preceding note one half of its value. The second dot in turn adds one half of this addition. Thus:

The eighth-note with two dots, subtracted from a quarter, leaves a new rhythmic value: the *thirty-second;* while the double-dotted sixteenth, subtracted from the eighth, leaves the *sixty-fourth.*

NOTATION: (1) The thirty-second is written thus: ♬ , or with beams: ♬ etc. The sixty-fourth: ♬ , ♬ . The respective rests are: ♯ and ♯ . The beams of thirty-seconds are grouped in sixteenths, eighths, or quarters: ♬ ♬ ♬ ♬ etc.: those of sixty-fourths in thirty-seconds, sixteenths, eighths, or quarters, in all cases with subdivisions which show clearly the beats and their metric structure: ♬ ♬ ♬ ♬ etc. Thus:

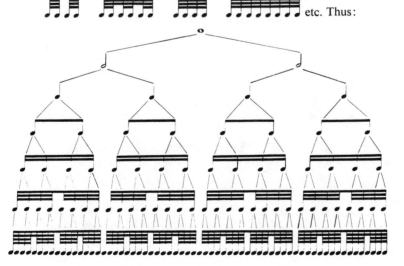

[77]

(2) Theoretically further subdivisions are possible, and in fact smaller values than the $\frac{1}{64}$ are exceptionally used $(\frac{1}{128})$.

Question: What is the number of

(a) ♪ in: $\dot{\downarrow}$ ....., $\mathbf{o}$ ....., $\dot{\downarrow}$ ....., $\dot{♪}$ ...., $\dot{\downarrow}\,♪$ .....?

(b) ♪ in: $\dot{\downarrow}$ ....., $\dot{\downarrow}$ ....., $\mathbf{o}\cdot$ ....., $\dot{\downarrow}$ ....., $\dot{♪}$ .....?

(Fill in.)

NOTATION: (1) For fast tempi the following terms are used:
    Allegro—Schnell—Animé = gay, quick;
    Vivace—Lebhaft—Vif = lively;
    Presto—Eilig—Vite, Rapide = fast.

(2) An Italian term is made stronger by the addition of the suffix *-issimo:* weaker by *-ino, -etto:*

    Adagissimo = slower than *Adagio;*
    Prestissimo = faster than *Presto;*
    Andantino = not as slow as *Andante;*
    Larghetto = not as broad as *Largo;*
    Allegretto = not as fast or energetic as *Allegro.*

(3) *Più*—[in German expressed by the suffix *-er*]—*plus* = more;
    Meno—weniger—moins = less;
    non troppo—nicht zu—pas trop = not too;
    Più presto—eiliger—plus vite = faster;
    Meno allegro—weniger schnell—moins vite = less fast;
    Adagio non troppo—nicht zu langsam—pas trop lent = not too slow.

—— EXERCISE 28 ——

1. Play, count aloud:

Moderato

Non troppo vivace

[78]

Molto Adagio

(c) ³⁄₈

1 and 2 and 3 and

More difficult:

Andante

(d) ⁴⁄₄

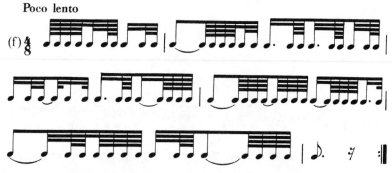

2. Sing, counting mentally:

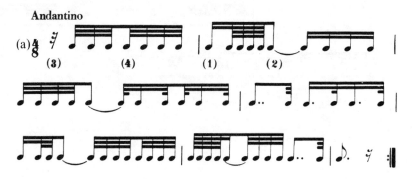

[80]

More difficult:

NOTATION: When after a *D.C. al segno* (𝄋 or ⊕) the piece continues, you first go back to the beginning as indicated by the *D.C.*, and when you reach the *segno* you skip to the part after the *D.C.*

Molto Adagio

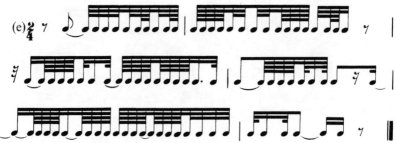

3. Invent similar examples.

—— DICTATION 27

B. Action in Space

The lower region of our tone system
(range of the men's voices, Tenor and Bass, and below)

NOTATION: (1) The tones of the lower region are written in the *Bass clef:*

𝄢 This clef is an *f*-clef.

(*Question:* What kind of clef is the 𝄞 ?)

It is written on the fourth line and marks the place of "small *f*":

𝄢 𝅝 = 𝄞

The notes of the *small octave* are: 𝄢 𝅝 𝅝 𝅝 𝅝 𝅝 𝅝

                                       c   d   e   f   g   a   b

(2) The notes of the next lower octave (*great octave*) are written with capital letters:

𝄢 𝅝 𝅝 𝅝 𝅝 𝅝 𝅝 𝅝

          C D E F G A B

(3) For the notes of the one-lined octave we depend (as we did for the high notes in 𝄞) on ledger lines. Compare the following notes in: 𝄢 with their equivalents in 𝄞

[82]

In reading bass clef notation don't determine the meaning of the notes by comparing them with notes written in treble clef! Get used at once to the fact that each clef has its independent existence. For example, the note *c'*

has its name and meaning through its position in an *f*-clef

relationship, and not by transposition of a similar-looking note in a *g*-clef

relationship. Not:

—— **EXERCISE 29** ——

1. Name the following notes:

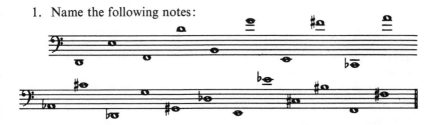

2. Play on the piano:

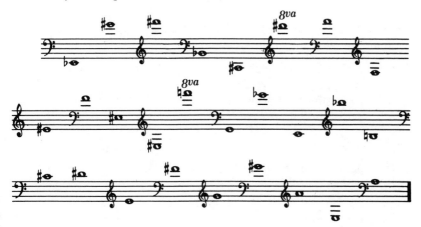

The dominant (mentioned in Chapter V) of a major scale is always the fifth degree of the scale. Its distance (or *interval*) from the tonic is called a *perfect fifth.*

The subdominant is always the fourth degree. The interval it forms with the tonic is called a *perfect fourth.*

Perfect fifth and perfect fourth, added up, complement each other to form the interval of an octave.

A perfect fifth *downward* from a tonic brings one to the subdominant;

a perfect fourth downward, to the dominant:

This means that the perfect fifth and the perfect fourth have a mutually reversible relation: a fifth upward is the *inversion* of a fourth downward from the same starting tone.

Or, what amounts to the same thing: the inversion of any interval smaller than an octave is equal to the difference between that interval and an octave.

—— EXERCISE 30 ——

1. On which of the seven degrees (tones) of a major scale can you build without changing any of the scale-tones:

   (a) a perfect fifth upward?
   (b) a perfect fourth upward?
   (c) a perfect fourth downward?
   (d) a perfect fifth downward?

2. Name the tones that lie

   (a) a perfect fifth above
   (b) a perfect fourth above
   (c) a perfect fourth below
   (d) a perfect fifth below
   each of the following notes (name tone and octave):

3. Sing, with its name, the tone that lies a perfect fifth above each of the following tones. Procedure:

First play the tone on the piano; then hit the fifth mentally; finally sing it, thus:

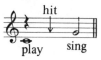

For men's voices, play and sing this example one octave lower.

4. Play and sing in the same manner the tone that lies a perfect fourth above each of the following notes:

In all vocal exercises from this point on, women's voices sing one octave higher whenever ")ː is used. In this case it is recommended that the higher octave be added to the tones played, in order to bridge the gap between a tone in the bass region and a high voice, and thus to facilitate hitting the tone to be sung.

5. Play and sing in the same manner the tones that lie a perfect fifth above the upper tones in the following chords (for men's voices play one octave lower):

[85]

Now sing the tones a perfect fourth above the upper tones.

Additional obstacle for these and all similar exercises: Have the chord played by someone else, and sing the tone without seeing the music.

NOTATION: (1) Combinations of stemmed notes can be written with a single stem, provided all the notes in the group have the same value. The common stem is that of the note most distant from the middle line:

Ambiguous cases: Downward stems preferred:

(2) Sometimes the course of different voices has to be marked on one single staff, or complex chords have to be made more legible. This is done by using upward and downward stems simultaneously:

(3) Sometimes tones a whole- or half-step apart are sounded simultaneously. Such pairs, either alone or as part of a chord, are usually written:

(a) when an upward stem is used, the higher note to the right of its neighbor and not in line with the other chord tones:

(b) when a downward stem is used, the lower note to the left and not in line with the other chord tones:

(c) when there is no stem (whole-notes), in the position that an appropriate upward or downward stem would require. (See the examples on the opposite page.)

[86]

Play and sing the tones a perfect fourth above the upper tones:

Now the tones a perfect fifth above the middle tones:

Now the tones a perfect fourth below the lowest tones:

6. Invent similar exercises.

—— *DICTATION 29*

C. Coordinated Action

—— EXERCISE 31 ——

1. Play on the piano, counting aloud. Name the keys of the examples.

Moderato assai

(a)

[87]

Allegretto

Andante con moto

More difficult:

Vivace

2. Sing. While singing add the accidentals of the key marked before each example.

Allegro assai in F♯ major

(b)

Lento in A♭ major

(c)

More difficult:

Moderato

(d)

(e)

Allegro in B major

—— *DICTATION 30*

CHAPTER VIII

A. Action in Time

Even in a series of sounds identical in every respect recurring at uniform time-intervals, the ear tends to hear regular groupings. It takes some of the sounds as more important than others, and thus hears the entire series as undulating between *accented* and *unaccented* beats.

This sort of accent (*metric* accent) which is determined by our feelings and not by any objective difference in the sounds themselves, is essentially different from the other kind of accent (*dynamic*) mentioned in Exercise 16, which is caused simply by the application of increased force. Frequently—especially in music of simple structure—the two types of accent coincide, and reinforce each other.

Music is generally composed in such a way that our perceptive faculty is not left in doubt about where the metric accents should be felt: proportions of rhythmic* (formal) length, the curves of melodic lines, and the distribution of harmonic functions serve as guides for our analytical hearing. But when all these guides are absent, as in the regular series of identical sounds mentioned above, we have a certain freedom to direct our hearing: we can understand such a series as subdivided into groups of two or three beats.

*The distinction between the two temporal factors of rhythm and meter can easily be comprehended by comparing their workings to the part played by the time element in our everyday life.

On the one hand there is the boundless and continuous stream of time-intervals in which our actions follow one another, the duration of each determined only by its character, purpose, speed, and intensity. This corresponds to musical *rhythm*, which has countless possibilities of combining tones and rests of various lengths with melodic lines and harmonic combinations. What characterizes musical rhythm is infinite variety, ruled by higher laws of construction and determined by the power of esthetic judgment and choice.

Meter, on the other hand, corresponds to the measurements of time invented by man or derived by him from natural events—divisions of time into distinct and proportionally related intervals (years, months, weeks, hours, minutes, etc.). Closely depending on our physical functions (e.g., pulse), meter provides the scheme of beats and counterbeats, accents and relaxations, without which no harmonic or melodic construction can be conceived.

Rhythm weaves freely in and out around the schematic divisions of meter, reinforcing or opposing these divisions. The inter-relations of these two temporal elements, in infinitely varying degrees of attraction and repulsion, form one of the important means by which music is created.

In two-beat groups, one of the beats is always felt as accented (*Arsis*) while the other makes the impression of unaccented relaxation (*Thesis*). The group may begin with either one:

In three-beat groups, the accent is felt on one of the beats while the other two seem unaccented:

In this context you will observe that the bar-line, which until now we have considered nothing but a symbol of temporal classification, has a higher purpose: it informs us about the metric order of tones, since it marks the place of the metric accent (which it always precedes).

——EXERCISE 32 ——

1. Clap a number of beats (about 20) and try, without clapping some beats louder than others, to direct your attention so as to understand them as divided into

   (a) $\frac{2}{4}$ ($\frac{2}{2}$, $\frac{2}{8}$) starting with the accent
   (b) $\frac{2}{4}$ ($\frac{2}{2}$, $\frac{2}{8}$) starting with the up-beat
   (c) $\frac{3}{4}$ ($\frac{3}{2}$, $\frac{3}{8}$) starting with the accent
   (d) $\frac{3}{4}$ ($\frac{3}{2}$, $\frac{3}{8}$) starting with one up-beat
   (e) $\frac{3}{4}$ ($\frac{3}{2}$, $\frac{3}{8}$) starting with two up-beats.

2. Clap, as before. Mark the metric accents by dynamic accents (tapping with your foot).

   In the following exercises you beat time according to the conventional patterns for conducting.

   The pattern for two-beat groups follows this scheme:

 which in the movement of the conducting hand looks approximately like:

Pattern for three-beat groups:

To give others the signal to start a piece one has to give one preparatory beat before the first actual beat. In fast tempo the preparatory beat
has the full value of a beat; in slow tempo, half of a beat; and in very
slow tempo even less.

Examples:

For a piece

    (a) beginning on the first beat in $\frac{3}{4}$

    (b) beginning on the second beat in $\frac{2}{4}$

    (c) beginning on the second beat in $\frac{3}{4}$

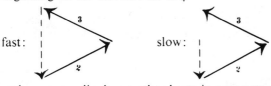

and correspondingly on other beats in any meter.

A fermata is indicated by slowly moving the hand in the direction of
the beat it falls on. If after the fermata the piece continues without
interruption, the next beat follows immediately after the fermata beat;
but if the fermata ends a piece or a section of it, the fermata beat has to
be cut off by a short concluding motion of the conducting hand.

Examples:

A beat following such a concluding motion must again be preceded by
a preparatory beat.

Sing the following melodic lines and divide them into groups of two beats; then into groups of three. Instead of clapping or tapping, beat time in the patterns given.

Example for beating time at the beginning of the next piece:

It is obvious that the application of different meters places the metric accents of the preceding pieces on different tones. This shifting of the metric accent sometimes causes the so-called *Syncopation* ("cutting up"), in which the metric accent, instead of coinciding with the beginning of a tone, occurs later in its duration:

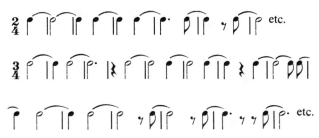

In singing and playing syncopated patterns one usually emphasizes the contradiction of meter and tone-rhythm by putting dynamic accents on the beginnings of the syncopated tones. Thus the metric accents can only be conceived by comparison with the context of normal (unsyncopated) patterns. Thus sing:

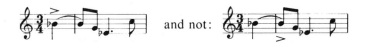

and not:

Syncopations may also occur, in note-values *shorter* than the beat unit, when one fraction of such a note-value comes before a beat and the remaining part after, no matter whether the beat is metrically accented or not:

[97]

2. Indicate in Exercises 10 to 31 all the syncopations you can find.

In analogy to the function of beats in the basic metric two-beat and three-beat groups, these groups themselves can be used as constituent elements in *compound* metric patterns. Hence a compound group can be constructed on a basis of two or three elements, which in turn can consist of two-beat or three-beat patterns:

 etc.

In these compound groups the order of metric accents is, on a larger scale, the same as in the two-beat and three-beat groups: in a compound consisting of two elements only, one element has the metric accent (order: heavy-light or light-heavy); in a compound with three elements one heavy group is associated with two light groups.

There is, however, a slight metric difference between the structure of simple-beat groups and that of compound patterns. For since, in spite of the dominating power of the "heavy" element in a compound metric pattern, the original accents in the "light" constituent groups are not completely suppressed, they will still be felt as accents, although in a reduced, subordinate degree.

$>$ = principal metric accent

$-$ = subordinate metric accent.

The following compound patterns are possible:

2+2; 2+2+2; 2+2+2+2; 3+3; 3+3+3; 3+3+3+3;

furthermore, combinations of 2 and 3, such as:

2+3; 3+2+2 etc.,

[98]

which will be discussed in Chapter X.

The statement on page 94 concerning the bar-line was, although useful, necessarily incomplete. Here is its complete form: The bar-line indicates the position of the *main* accent; the positions of secondary accents have to be deduced from the time-signature—as the next paragraph (on notation) will show.

NOTATION: (1) These compound groups appear in notation as follows:

(a) Groups of which the constituent is

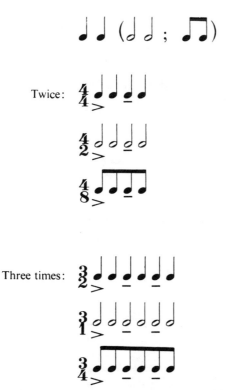

Three times:

(this would mean a tempo slower than that of the normal $\frac{3}{4}$, since in fast tempo the subordinate accents cannot be understood).

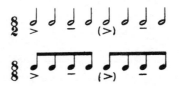

(The last three are used mostly in the form of $\frac{4}{4}$, $\frac{4}{2}$, and $\frac{4}{8}$, since the larger forms would necessitate the establishment of three degrees of metric accents—and this reaches beyond the limit of metric arrangement into the realm of form.)

(b) Groups of which the constituent is

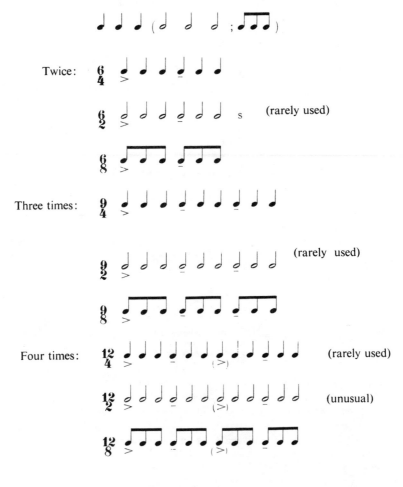

[100]

In order to avoid the above-mentioned introduction of three degrees of metric accents it is better to use measures having the numerator 12 only when the meter can be understood as a form of $\frac{4}{4}$ ($\frac{4}{2}$, $\frac{4}{8}$). In this case three eighths in a $\frac{12}{8}$ measure correspond to two eighths in a $\frac{4}{4}$ measure—namely one fourth of the whole group. This reduces the accents in the measure to two: one on each half, while the accents of the third degree (on the 4th and 10th eighths) disappear. If an equation $\frac{12}{8} = \frac{4}{4}$ is not possible, it is preferable to divide the measure in two, and write $\frac{6}{8}$ ($\frac{6}{2}$ or $\frac{6}{4}$) instead of $\frac{12}{8}$ ($\frac{12}{2}$ or. $\frac{12}{4}$). More about such equations in the next Chapter.

(2) In exceptional cases the basic patterns ♪♩ and ♪♪♩ may be used as the constituents of compound meters:

ıt it is obvious that the order of accents can be understood only in slow tempo, which leads us to consider whether the legibility of such notation is not unnecessarily complicated, owing to the contradiction between the inherently short value of one sixteenth part of a whole and its actually long duration in slow tempo.

(3) Note that in musical measures fractions with the numerator 6 are always bipartite while measures with the same number of beats but with the numerator 3 are tripartite. Bipartite are: 4, 6, 8, 12; tripartite: 3 and 9. For this reason we have to write a $2+2+2$ compound based on ♩ as $\frac{3}{2}$ and not as $\frac{6}{4}$. The same is true for $\frac{3}{4}$ and $\frac{6}{8}$, $\frac{3}{1}$ and $\frac{6}{2}$.

Sing, beating time:

(a) The patterns for $\frac{4}{4}$, $\frac{4}{2}$, $\frac{4}{8}$ are:

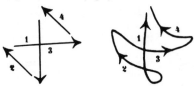

Moderato

(b) $\frac{4}{8}$ can also be treated as a $\frac{2}{4}$ with subdivisions:

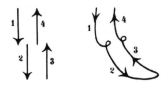

Adagio

(c) $\frac{3}{2}, \frac{3}{8}, \frac{3}{4}$ are treated either as a regular three-beat group (see p. 94), or with subdivisions:

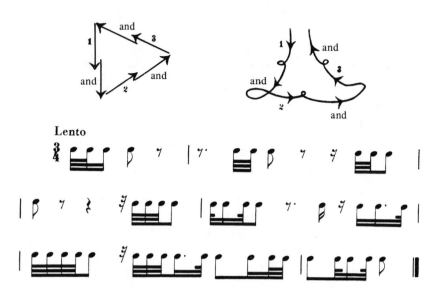

Lento

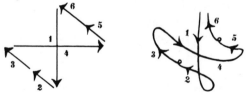

(d) $\frac{6}{4}, \frac{6}{2}, \frac{6}{8}$ are treated in fast tempo as a two-beat group (see p. 94), or in slow tempo thus:

Andantino

[103]

Presto

(e)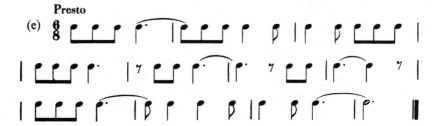

(f) $\frac{9}{4}$ and $\frac{9}{8}$ are treated in fast tempo as a three-beat group (see p. 94), or in slow tempo thus:

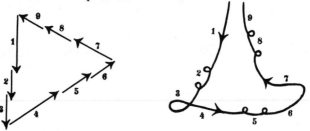

Allegro

Andante

(g)

(h) $\frac{12}{8}$ are treated in fast tempo as $\frac{4}{4}$ (see p. 102), or in slow tempo thus:

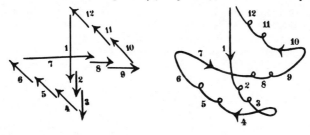

Moderato

NOTATION: (1) Undotted rests are always understood as bipartite metric structures, with the metric accent on the beginning. Hence:

(a) an undotted rest must not occur in a "syncopated" position.

(b) an undotted rest may represent the first two thirds of the tripartite subdivisions of any *compound* metric pattern:

(although the following

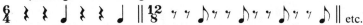

is also correct) but it is unusual to use it for the same purpose in *simple* tripartite constructions:

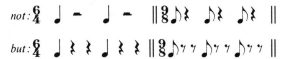

For filling out the last two thirds of any tripartite pattern (simple or compound), an undotted rest is not acceptable, since the inherent bipartite metric structure of the rest with its metric accent felt on the first half puts a contrasting and disturbing force against the metric accent of the tripartite group, represented by the preceding note:

(2) The half-measure rest in $\frac{12}{8}$ is  hence:

But: according to the

preceding rule (1a).

Similarly in $\frac{9}{8}$:  not:

B. Action in Space

The octave below C is called the *Contra Octave*.

NOTATION: (1) The tones of the Contra octave are written:

(2) In order to avoid the ledger lines one may use the *8va* sign (cf. p. 66):

The octave sign for the lower octave is sometimes written *8va bassa*
The octave sign for the higher octave (*8va-------*) is not used in **):

[106]

(3) Below ‚C the piano has three more keys in the *Sub-contra Octave:*
‚‚B,‚‚‚B flat (or ‚‚A sharp), ‚‚A; sometimes marked ₂B, ₂B flat (or ₂A sharp),
₂A.

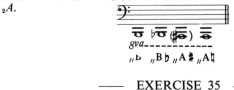

—— EXERCISE 35 ——

Play on the piano, naming tones and octaves:

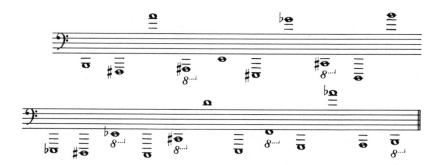

—— *DICTATION 31*

The space between the dominant and the leading tone of a major
scale is called a *Major Third.*

N.B. All intervals from now on are counted upwards except in
cases where the other direction is specifically mentioned.

Question: On what other degrees of the major scale can you find major
thirds?

The interval between the second degree and the subdominant in a
major scale is called a *Minor Third.*

Question: On what other degrees of the major scale can you find minor
thirds?

—— EXERCISE 36 ——

1. Play the following tones and sing tones a major third above them.
Performance as described in Exercise 30. For men's voices, play and
sing one octave lower.

[107]

2. Play; sing the tones a minor third above:

3. Play; sing the tones a major third *below:*

4. Play; sing the tones a minor third below. Women's voices one octave higher (cf. Ex. 30).

5. Play; sing the tones a major third above the upper tones:

6. Play; sing the tones a minor third above the upper tones:

7. Play; sing the tones a major third below the lowest tones:

8. Play; sing the tones a minor third below the lowest tones. For women's voices: sing and play one octave higher—but don't double the chords in the lower octave.

Following the rules given on page 84 you can invert both thirds.
Invert the major third; the result is the *Minor Sixth.*
Question: On what degrees of a major scale can you find minor sixths?

Invert the minor third; the result is the *Major Sixth.*
Question: On what degrees of a major scale can you find major sixths?

The fact that the inversion of the *major* third is the *minor* sixth and that of the *minor* third is the *major* sixth leads us to the general statement that the inversions of all major intervals are minor, and vice versa. Perfect intervals, however, remain perfect in their inversions (perfect fifth—perfect fourth).

—— EXERCISE 37 ——

1. Play the following tones; sing tones a minor sixth above. Performance as described before. Treatment of men's and women's voices as in the preceding exercise.

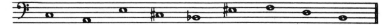

2. Play; sing tones a major sixth above:

3. Play; sing tones a minor sixth *below:*

4. Play; sing tones a major sixth below:

5. Play; sing tones a minor sixth above the upper tones:

6. Play; sing tones a major sixth above the upper tones:

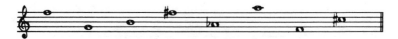

7. Play; sing tones a major sixth below the lowest tones:

8. Play; sing tones a minor sixth below the lowest tones:

—— DICTATION 32

C. Coordinated Action

—— EXERCISE 38 ——

1. Play on the piano; count aloud:

Allegro

2. Sing, beating time. While singing, add sharps or flats to certain tones, in order to realize the tonality marked at the beginning of each piece.

(a) Beat in $\frac{9}{8}$, beginning with the first beat, then beginning with the fourth, and finally with the seventh.

After this: beat in $\frac{12}{8}$, following the same procedure (first beat; fourth; seventh; tenth).

Andantino in A major

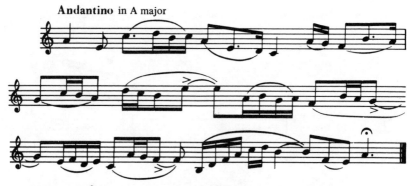

(b) Beat in $\frac{3}{2}$ (three ways), then in $\frac{4}{2}$ (four ways).

If a piece starts with a rest of short value, no special preparatory beat need be given: the beat on the rest itself serves as preparatory beat. In beating the following piece you have to start thus:

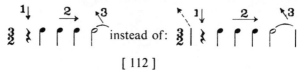

Allegro in D♭ major

(c) Beat in ♪ , taking a different eighth as starting point each time (six ways).

Lento in F♯ major

(d) Beat in ♩. , first in 6/4 (two ways), then in 9/4 (three ways).

Presto in B♭ major

1 *beat*

3. (a) Play a chord on the piano. Sing *c'*, hold it for a moment, then sing the C-major scale up and down. Thus:

Sing:

Play:

Chords to be played:

(b) Play and sing the same examples
one half-tone lower;
one half-tone higher.

This procedure (shifting of a complete tonality to another tone-level) is called *Transposition*.

(c) Invent similar exercises.

—— *DICTATION 33*

CHAPTER IX

A. Action in Time

The construction of compound measures was based on *multiplication*—doubling and tripling of certain metric units. But looking back from the established compound measures we can also regard these compound results as units and the shorter values as their partials. Thus we can state that *division* into two or three parts is the reverse of this multiplication, and hence can also be used in establishing metric devices.

In fact, we have used it already for this purpose, as a glimpse at page 77 will show. But there we used only the division by 2 or its multiples 4, 8, 16, etc., and stated that our notation provides no equally simple and accurate means for expressing other divisions.

Division by 3, however, is easily possible if we take a dotted note as the divisible unit. Then: ♩. ($\frac{3}{8}$) = one beat, and ♪($\frac{1}{8}$) = one-third of a beat. But if we wish to divide this ♪ ($\frac{1}{8}$) in turn by 3 (producing one-ninth of a beat), how can we notate this further division (= $\frac{1}{24}$)?

Division of a dotted note by 2, although possible by the continued use of smaller dotted values (♩. [$\frac{3}{4}$] = ♩. ♩.[2 × $\frac{3}{8}$], = ♫♫♫♫.

[4 × $\frac{3}{16}$], = ♫♫♫♫ ♫♫♫♫.[8 × $\frac{3}{32}$]) is cumbersome to read, and

hence, except for its first step, it is rarely used. And apart from this difficulty, it is almost impossible in the adaption of notation to practical music to use units of different graphic forms but identical duration in one and the same part of a piece: the use of ♩ and ♩. together as equivalent representatives of a single value is not possible without causing the greatest confusion, even in writing a simple $\frac{4}{4}$ measure.

NOTATION: In order to avoid this confusion and still find in our uniformly bipartite notation a means of expressing the metric values of thirds, ninths, etc., and even of such complicated fractions as fifths, sevenths, elevenths, etc., we use the following device:

We symbolize these values (or multiples of them) by the next longer values for which we have notes: ♩ ($\frac{1}{2}$) for $\frac{1}{3}$, ♩ ($\frac{1}{4}$) for $\frac{1}{5}$, $\frac{1}{6}$, or $\frac{1}{7}$, ♪ ($\frac{1}{8}$) for $\frac{1}{9}$, $\frac{1}{10}$, ... $\frac{1}{15}$, and so on, and show by a numeral how the metric unit is being divided, and by a bracket which notes or rests go to make up the metric unit.

[115]

The bracket can be omitted when the higher metric unit is already indicated by a beam.

Thus the following patterns are made possible:

$\circ = $ [notation: three notes bracketed 3] $\left[\begin{smallmatrix}3\\3\end{smallmatrix}\right]$, [notation: six notes bracketed 6] $\left[\begin{smallmatrix}6\\6\end{smallmatrix}\right]$,

[notation: five notes bracketed 5] $\left|\begin{smallmatrix}5\\5\end{smallmatrix}\right|$, [notation: seven notes bracketed 7] $\left[\begin{smallmatrix}7\\7\end{smallmatrix}\right]$ etc.

[notation] $= $ [notation bracketed 3] $\left[\begin{smallmatrix}3\\6\end{smallmatrix}\right]$, [notation bracketed 6] $\left[\begin{smallmatrix}6\\12\end{smallmatrix}\right]$,

[notation bracketed 5] $\left[\begin{smallmatrix}5\\10\end{smallmatrix}\right]$, [notation bracketed 7] $\left[\begin{smallmatrix}7\\14\end{smallmatrix}\right]$ etc.

[notation] $=$ [notation bracketed 3] $\left[\begin{smallmatrix}3\\12\end{smallmatrix}\right]$, [notation bracketed 6] $\left[\begin{smallmatrix}6\\24\end{smallmatrix}\right]$,

[notation bracketed 5] $\left[\begin{smallmatrix}5\\20\end{smallmatrix}\right]$, [notation bracketed 7] $\left|\begin{smallmatrix}7\\28\end{smallmatrix}\right|$ etc.

[notation] $=$ [notation bracketed 3] $\left[\begin{smallmatrix}3\\24\end{smallmatrix}\right]$, [notation bracketed 6] $\left[\begin{smallmatrix}6\\48\end{smallmatrix}\right]$,

[notation bracketed 5] $\left[\begin{smallmatrix}5\\40\end{smallmatrix}\right]$, [notation bracketed 7] $\left[\begin{smallmatrix}7\\56\end{smallmatrix}\right]$ etc.

and similarly for ♪ and ♬

Note that here too the distinction between bipartite and tripartite division (as mentioned on page 101) is valid: ⌐3⌐ is tripartite, while ⌐6⌐ is bipartite and consequently can also be written as a double ⌐3⌐, thus:

♩ = [notation with 6] or [notation with 3, 3]

The tripartite relationship ♩ : ♪ is written thus: [notation with 3]

Consequently: ♩:♪ = [notation with 3] but frequently we find this latter group-

[116]

ing (and the corresponding relations ♪ ♫ ♫ ♫) written rather inconsistently. The following figure:

$\frac{2}{4}$ ♩♩♩ (or  ♩♩♩) is frequently

written: ♩♩♩

In slow tempo the distinction between the two different subordinate accents spoils the intended effect, but in a fairly fast tempo these minor accents cannot be felt; hence the quasi-justification of such careless forms.

In meters where a *dotted note* fills one whole measure, subdivisions are written as follows:

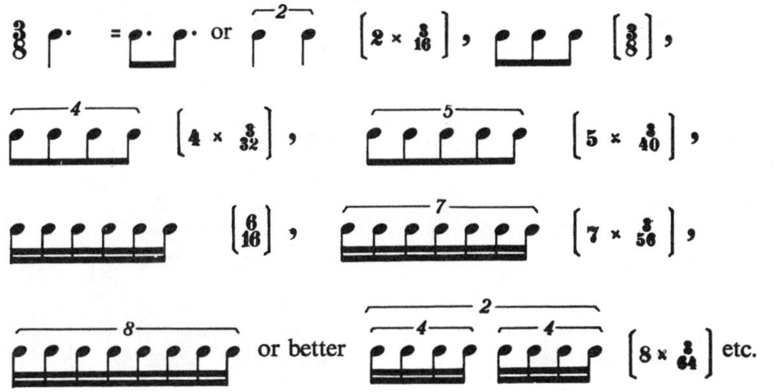

Correspondingly in $\frac{3}{4}$ and $\frac{3}{2}$.

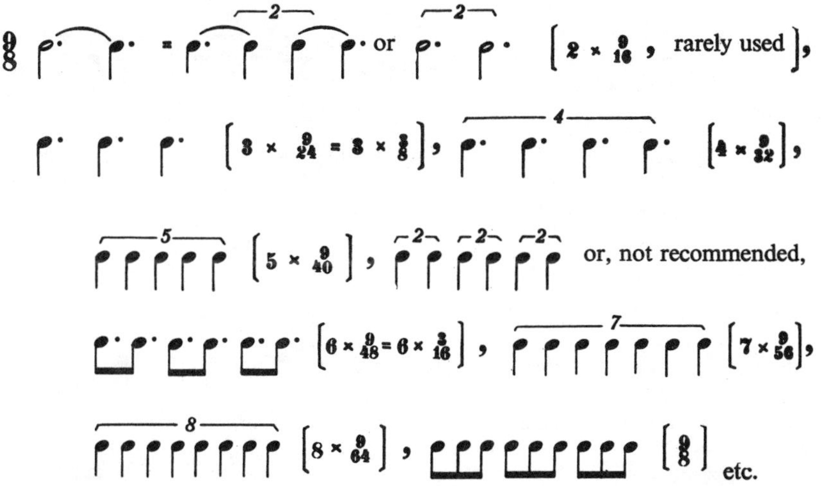

$$\left[2 \times \tfrac{6}{16} = 2 \times \tfrac{3}{8}\right], \quad \text{or}$$

$$\left[3 \times \tfrac{6}{24} = 3 \times \tfrac{2}{8}\right], \quad \text{or} \quad \text{or, not recommended}$$

$$\left[4 \times \tfrac{6}{32} = 4 \times \tfrac{3}{16}\right], \quad \left[5 \times \tfrac{6}{40}\right],$$

$$\left[\tfrac{6}{8}\right], \quad \left[7 \times \tfrac{6}{56}\right],$$

or, not recommended, $$\left[8 \times \tfrac{6}{64} = 8 \times \tfrac{3}{32}\right],$$

$$\left[9 \times \tfrac{6}{72}\right], \quad \left[10 \times \tfrac{6}{80}\right],$$

$$\left[11 \times \tfrac{6}{88}\right], \quad \left[\tfrac{12}{16}\right] \text{ etc.}$$

NOTE: Frequently one finds the division by 4 written thus:

$$\tfrac{6}{8} \quad \text{or} \quad \text{instead of} \quad \text{or}$$

The latter notation is always preferable, since it follows the general rule that for fractions other than plain $\tfrac{1}{2}$, $\tfrac{1}{4}$, $\tfrac{1}{8}$, etc., the next *longer* note-value ought to be used (see p. 115).

Correspondingly in $\tfrac{3}{4}$ and $\tfrac{6}{2}$.

$$\tfrac{12}{8} \quad \left[2 \times \tfrac{6}{8}\right], \quad \text{or}$$

$3 \times \tfrac{12}{24} = 3 \times \tfrac{4}{8}$, very rarely used, and possible only in very fast tempo,

[116b]

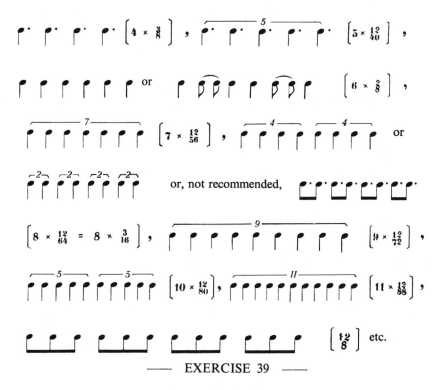

—— EXERCISE 39 ——

Construct the divisions of ♩· ($\frac{3}{2}$, $\frac{6}{4}$), ♩· ($\frac{3}{4}$), ♩·($\frac{6}{16}$), ♩· ($\frac{9}{4}$), without looking at the preceding paragraph.

The names of these newly established values are: duplets (⌐2⌐), triplets (⌐3⌐), quadruplets, and so forth up to decuplets (⌐10⌐) and even smaller subdivisions. But some of these terms are so awkward (linguistically) that they are hardly ever used, and various makeshifts are resorted to in order to avoid them.

NOTATION: (1) It is obvious that there is no essential difference between

[117]

and there are many other cases where the mutual dependence of time-signature and note-values cause ambiguity in writing. Merely questions of practicability (additional work in writing the symbols for triplets, etc.) and sometimes minute distinctions in the determination of tempo ($\frac{9}{8}$ is generally felt as a slower tempo than $\frac{3}{4}$—without any obvious reason!) influence a composer in his choice.

(2) Continuous tripartite (and smaller) subdivisions of triplets show clearly the weakness of these makeshift constructions:

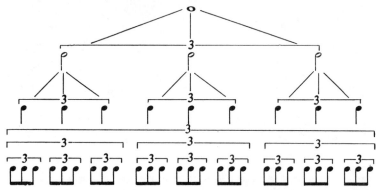

Here the value of $\frac{1}{27}$ has to be written by the value that originally represented $\frac{1}{8}$! Although such a case may rarely occur, and normally twenty-sevenths not in connection with a preceding twofold triple division have to be written as sixteenths (these being the next larger value), this monstrosity is nevertheless theoretically justified.

—— EXERCISE 40 ——

1. Sing, beating time:

[118]

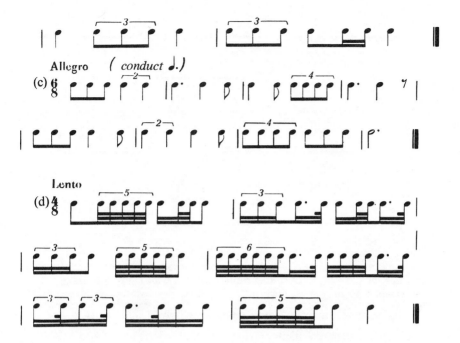

2. Invent similar examples.
3. Sing; let another person tap the rhythms indicated in the second line; a third person may beat time. (Perhaps you can beat time yourself.)

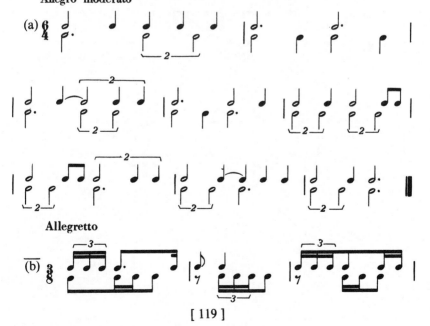

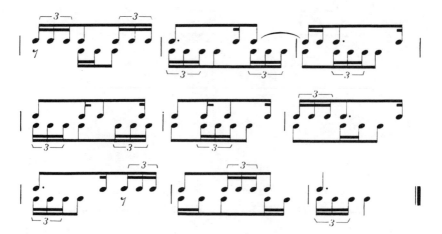

NOTATION: In pieces like the preceding one the number for the triplet can easily be omitted, since in this context a beam with a group of three notes attached can only mean a triplet. In other divisions in which beams substitute for brackets the numeral may be omitted similarly (♩ ♪♪♪♪ ♩ = ♪♪♪♪♪), especially when repetitions make the numeral superfluous.

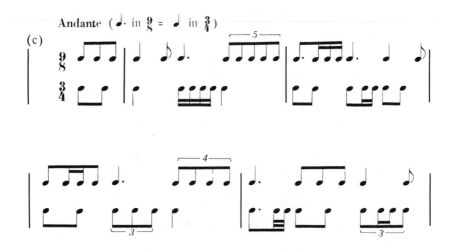

In beating triplets that are not subdivisions of the beat-unit of a meter, but are the tripartite division of two beats combined (♩♩♩ in ⁴⁄₄), certain difficulties arise when in slow tempo they are opposed to a group of regular beats, e.g., ♩♩♩ in ⁴⁄₄.

The conductor usually beats the regular rhythm indicated by the time-signature, but the player or singer of the triplet has to arrange his group so that the second of the regular beats falls in the middle of the second tone of the triplet. This can easily be proved by bringing the fractions that express the two rhythmical patterns to a common denominator:

$$\frac{3}{6} = \frac{6}{12}$$
$$\frac{2}{4} = \frac{6}{12}$$

By the same operation we can determine the proper distribution of other opposed rhythmic groups in one meter:

$$\frac{3}{6} = \frac{12}{24}$$
$$\frac{4}{8} = \frac{12}{24}$$

$$\frac{3}{6} = \frac{15}{30}$$
$$\frac{5}{10} = \frac{15}{30}$$

[122]

4. Invent similar examples.

—— *DICTATION 34*

B. Action in Space

The interval between subdominant and dominant (a whole tone) is called a *Major Second.*

—— EXERCISE 41 ——

1. Play the following tones and sing the tones a major second above them. Performance as described in Exercise 30. For men's voices sing and play one octave lower.

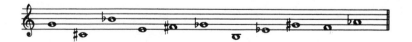

2. Play; sing the tones a major second *below:*

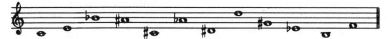

3. Play; sing the tones a major second above the upper tones:

4. Play; sing the tones a major second below the lowest tones. For women's voices, sing and play one octave higher.

The half-tone step, as it appears between leading-tone and tonic, is called a *Minor Second.*

—— EXERCISE 42 ——

1. Play; sing (as before) the tones a minor second above the played tones:

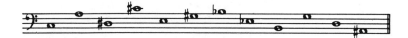

2. Play; sing the tones a minor second *below:*

3. Play; sing the tones a minor second above the upper tones:

4. Play; sing the tones a minor second below the lowest tones:

The inversions of seconds are sevenths, and, in accordance with the statement on page 109 the inversion of the major second is the *Minor Seventh*, and that of the minor second the *Major Seventh*.

The minor seventh is to be found in the major scale between dominant and subdominant (upwards), while the major seventh is the interval between tonic and leading tone (upwards).

Question: Where else in the major scale can you find minor and major sevenths?

—— EXERCISE 43 ——

1. Play and sing as before. Sing the tones a minor seventh above the played tones.

2. Play; sing the tones a major seventh above:

3. Play; sing the tones a minor seventh *below:*

4. Play; sing the tones a major seventh below:

5. Play; sing the tones a minor seventh above the upper tones:

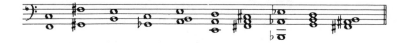

6. Play; sing the tones a major seventh above the upper tones:

7. Play; sing the tones a minor seventh below the lowest tones:

8. Play; sing the tones a major seventh *below* the lowest tones:

       — *DICTATION 35*

[126]

C. Coordinated Action

—— EXERCISE 44 ——

1. Play on the piano. One of your fellow students (or the teacher) may clap the rhythms below the lines; another may conduct the beats, if you cannot do so yourself.

Transpose the above piece one tone lower, playing it in G major (without writing it out!).

Play this piece one tone higher.

Play this piece in E major and in G major.

Play the above piece in G-flat major and B-flat major.

Try other transpositions of the preceding pieces, as well as of pieces in earlier exercises.

NOTATION: (1) The tempo is not always constant throughout a piece. Terms for intensifying or reducing a pre-established tempo are:

accelerando (*accel.*)—*schneller werden, beschleunigen*—*accélérer* = accelerate;
stringendo (*string.*)—*drängend*—*en pressant* = becoming faster and more
intense;

più mosso—bewegter—plus animé = faster;
ritardando (rit., ritard.)—langsamer werden—ralentissant = retard;
rallentando (rall.)—zurückhalten—ralentir, ralentissant = slacken, retard;
allargando—verbreitern—-élargissant = broaden;
meno mosso—weniger bewegt—moins vite = less fast;
ritenuto (riten.)—zurückgehalten—retenu = held back.

The gradation of a change over a passage of some length is marked:
poco a poco (—allmählich—peu à peu), with the appropriate adjective.

(2) The following terms mean a simultaneous reduction of tempo and loudness:
calando—nachlassen—en diminuant = decrease;
smorzando—verlöschen—en s'effaçant = dying away;
morendo—ersterben—en mourant = dying down.

(3) The restoration of the main tempo is marked by:

a tempo, or: *tempo primo.*

—— EXERCISE 45 ——

1. Sing and beat time. Have another person clap the rhythms marked below the melody. Beat time for each example, beginning at first with the first beat; then go through all forms of upbeat starts.

   (a) Conduct in ¾ (beat ♩), ⁶⁄₈ (beat ♩.), ⁹⁄₈ (beat ♩.), and ⁴⁄₄ (beat ♩). Watch the syncopations!

Transpose the above piece to D-flat major and F major.

[130]

Sometimes tones appear that do not belong to the key as expressed by the key-signature (see the *d"-flat* in the preceding example). As long as such new tones are not caused by chromatic alteration of the main tonal pillars (tonic, dominant, subdominant), and they do not distract the attention from more important tonal facts, no disturbance of tonality will result. Accumulation of these tones, however, especially at important places, is used as an artistic means to bring a tonality out of balance or replace it by another one (*Modulation*). Such devices are not used in these elementary exercises. (Cf. Exercise 27, c.)

(b) Beat time in $\frac{2}{8}$ (♪)) and $\frac{3}{8}$ (♪)):

Transpose to A major and C-sharp major.

(c) Beat time in $\frac{2}{4}$ (♩), $\frac{2}{2}$ (♩), $\frac{3}{2}$ (♩), $\frac{3}{4}$ (♩), $\frac{6}{4}$ (♩.), $\frac{6}{8}$ (♩.):

Transpose to C-flat major and E-flat major.

(d) Beat time in $\frac{6}{8}$, $\frac{9}{8}$, $\frac{12}{8}$, (♩.):

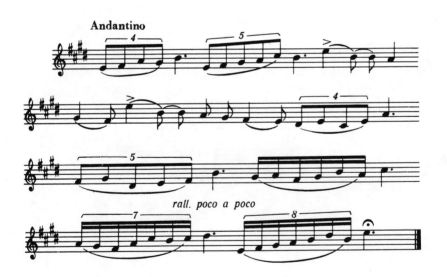

Transpose to D major and F-sharp major

2. Play chords on the piano, and sing the broken scale-lines.
   Easier for men's voices: sing one octave lower, play two octaves higher:

repeat more than once.

[133]

DICTATION 36

CHAPTER X

A. Action in Time

In the division of metrical units by 5, 7, etc., (quintuplets, septuplets, etc., of the preceding chapter) we already encountered certain deviations from the normal bipartite and tripartite metrical schemes.

But since division, as we know (see p. 115), can be replaced by multiplication, compound measures based on fractions with the numerators 5, 7, etc., are also possible.

This leads us to the construction of $\frac{5}{16}, \frac{5}{8}, \frac{5}{4}, \frac{5}{2}, \frac{7}{16}, \frac{7}{8}, \frac{7}{4}, \frac{7}{2}$. Theoretically, forms like $\frac{11}{4}, \frac{13}{8}$, etc., are also possible, but they are not practicable, since through sub-groupings these meters can be written in shorter and more legible forms ($\frac{11}{4}$ as $\frac{6}{4}$ | $\frac{5}{4}$; $\frac{13}{8}$ as $\frac{4}{8}$ | $\frac{5}{8}$ | $\frac{4}{8}$, etc.).

The accents in the 5- and 7-compounds are:

5: ⌐| | ⌐| | | (2 + 3)   or   ⌐| | | ⌐| | (3 + 2)

7: ⌐| | | ⌐| | | | (3 + 4)   or   ⌐| | | | ⌐| | | (4 + 3).

In slow tempo, the accents in a 7-compound may even be felt as:

⌐| | ⌐| | ⌐| | or   ⌐| | ⌐| ⌐| | |

and even:

⌐| ⌐| | ⌐| ⌐| |

NOTATION: In measures with ♪ or ♪ as the metric unit the distribution of accents can easily be shown by the position of the beams

(♪♪ ♪♪♪ , ♬♬ ♬). while use of the units ♩ and ♩ often leaves the performer without a hint as to where the accents are. If necessary, an auxiliary bar-line before the subordinate accent will contribute to the clarity of such cases:

$\frac{7}{4}$ ♪ ♪ ♪ ♪ ♪ ♪ | ♪ ♪ ♪ ♪ ♪

♪ ♪ ♪ ♪ ♪ ♪ ♪ |

Sometimes other irregular metric groupings occur, the notes of which add up to a regular compound with one of the higher numerators 8, 9, or 12 in its time-signature, but with the accents placed as in $\frac{5}{4}$ or $\frac{7}{4}$. Here auxiliary bar-lines are indispensable:

$$\frac{8}{4} \; \flat \; \flat \; | \; \flat \; \flat \; | \; \flat \; \flat \; | \; \flat \; \flat \; | \; \frac{9}{8} \; \text{♪♪♪♪} \; | \; \text{♪♪♪♪♪} \; | \; etc.$$

NOTATION: The relationship that exists between $\frac{6}{8}$ and $\frac{2}{4}$, $\frac{9}{8}$ and $\frac{3}{4}$, etc., we find again between $\frac{15}{8}$ and $\frac{5}{4}$, and consequently in all other compounds where

metric equations similar to $\frac{3}{12} = \frac{1}{4}$ (written: $\frac{3}{8} = \frac{1}{4}$, ♪. = ♪) are

used. Thus: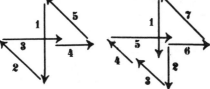

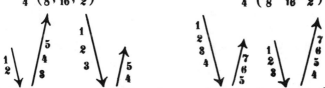

In beating time for all the aforementioned compound measures one generally divides them up into groups of 2, 3, or 4 beats, according to the position of their accents. Since in this case each accent, even a subordinate one, is indicated by a down-stroke, a certain ambiguity arises for singers and players following a conductor, in respect to the first beat of the measure. This can be avoided by conducting $\frac{5}{4}$ ($\frac{5}{8}$, $\frac{5}{16}$, $\frac{5}{2}$) and $\frac{7}{4}$ ($\frac{7}{8}$, $\frac{7}{16}$, $\frac{7}{2}$) thus:

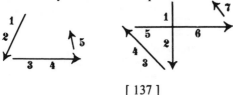

In very fast tempo they can be beaten as defective two-beat measures:

$\frac{5}{4}$ ($\frac{5}{8}$, $\frac{5}{16}$, $\frac{5}{2}$) $\frac{7}{4}$ ($\frac{7}{8}$, $\frac{7}{16}$, $\frac{7}{2}$)

Sometimes even conducting them as defective three-beat ($\frac{5}{4}$) or four-beat ($\frac{7}{4}$) measures may facilitate their performance:

[137]

— EXERCISE 46 —

1. Sing, beating time:

Allegretto

(a)  7/4

Andante

(b)  5/8

Presto

(c) 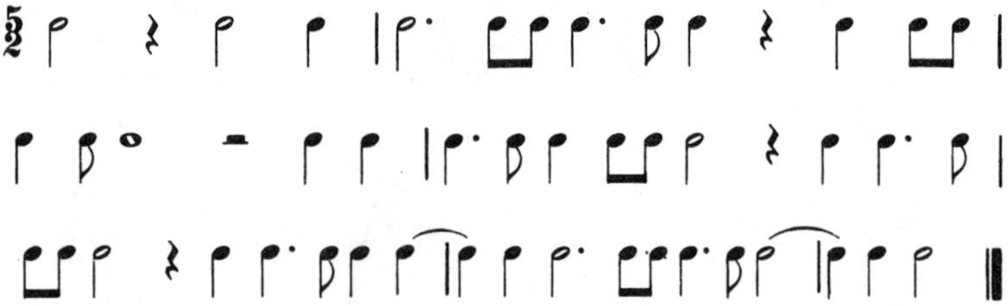 5/2

Allegro moderato

(d)  8/4

[138]

Larghetto

(e)

Allegro assai

(f)

2. Invent similar examples.

3. Sing, following instruction 3 on page 119:

Andante

(a)

Beat time first for the upper part, then for the lower:

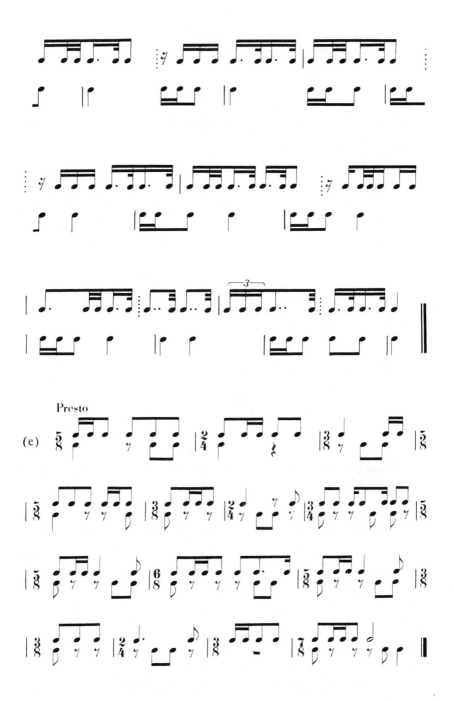

4. Invent similar examples.

—— *DICTATION 37*

B. Action in Space

NOTATION: For certain instruments whose range occupies the middle region of our tone-system, clefs are used which render unnecessary the frequent writing of ledger lines that the use of 𝄞 or 𝄢 would necessitate.

One of these is the *Alto Clef*, used for the low and middle region of the Viola. Originally conceived for the contralto voice (whose approximate range, as used in choral writing, it covers almost without ledger lines), it served also in notation for Alto Trombones and high Violas da gamba.

It is a *c′*-clef, marking the place of *c′* on the middle line of the staff:

Not more than two or three upper ledger lines are commonly used with the alto clef (for higher notes the 𝄞 is used), and it is almost never used for

notes lower than *c* :

—— EXERCISE 47 ——

1. Name the following notes. Keep in mind the remark on page 83 about reading clefs!

2. Play on the piano:

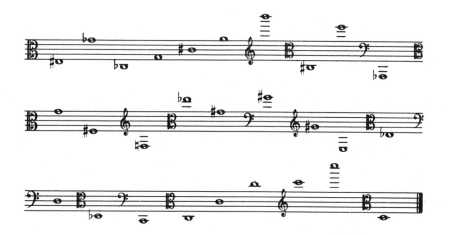

The major scale contains two more intervals, which in construction and character are rather different from all others. The one is the distance from the subdominant up to the leading tone, the other its inversion. The first is called *Augmented Fourth*, the second, *Diminished Fifth*.

in C major

In contradistinction to other intervals the original form and the inversion are almost alike: both consist of six half-tone steps, although the augmented fourth contains three whole tones of the scale in succession (1+1+1, as in C major:

$$f\underline{\quad}g\underline{\quad}a\underline{\quad}b)$$
$$1\quad 1\quad 1$$

—hence its name *Tritone* ("three tone")—while the diminished fifth is built on the scale steps $\frac{1}{2}+1+1+\frac{1}{2}$

(in C major:

$$b\underline{\quad}c\underline{\quad}d\underline{\quad}e\underline{\quad}f).$$
$$\tfrac{1}{2}\quad 1\quad 1\quad \tfrac{1}{2}$$

[143]

NOTATION: These intervals are augmented and diminished in respect to the perfect intervals from which they are derived. This can more easily be recognized by looking at the subdominant and leading tone of scales other than C major, as, for instance, A major:

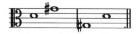

Here we see clearly that the tritone d'—$g\sharp'$ is an extended form of the perfect fourth d'—g', while the diminished fifth $g\sharp$—d' can be traced back to the perfect fifth g—d'.

This fact is caused merely by the imperfection of our notation, which has more than one symbol for each tone ($e\sharp = f, f\sharp = g\flat$). If notation were constructed along the same lines as the keyboard—i.e., with only one key ($=$ symbol) for each tone—no augmentation or diminution would exist.

On the piano the tritone and diminished fifth are the same (c—$f\sharp = c$—$g\flat$). But in a tuning based on the natural sizes of intervals (the "tempered" intervals on the piano, except for the octave, are slightly distorted; see the footnote on page 52) there is a difference. This can be felt in singing choral music or in playing ensemble music without keyboard instruments: here it will often occur that in order to produce the most satisfactory harmonic effect the function of a leading tone (its urge toward its tonic) has to be emphasized. That means that this tone will be played or sung somewhat sharper. Thus the tritone of which it is a part will be widened by the same small amount of space (called *Comma*) by which the complementary diminished fifth will be reduced.

Although the other intervals may also show slight variations of size, such variations will always be understood as deviations from a natural, normal size for each interval established in the physical fact of the overtone-series*. Tritone and diminished fifth have no such simple, normal, natural prototype. Theoretically we can construct upon one single tone an infinite number of tritones and diminished fifths, although the margin between a very narrow diminished fifth and an extremely wide tritone may not exceed $\frac{1}{4}$ tone.

Owing to this vagueness, it is difficult to sing a tritone or diminished fifth to a given tone unless additional tones make clear its melodic or harmonic meaning.

Both intervals lack the stability and independence of the perfect, major, and minor intervals. They lean towards their more stable neighbors, and have the tendency to "resolve" into one of them, either melod-

*In this book on elementary *technical* training we cannot occupy ourselves with the intricacies of tone-measurement and acoustical reasoning. See the special literature on this subject.

ically or harmonically. Thus the preferred melodic or harmonic sequels to a tritone or a diminished fifth are:

NOTATION: (1) In order to construct these two intervals on each of the basic tones and their raised or lowered derivations, we have to rely on two more accidentals:

×(*double sharp*) and ♭♭ (*double flat*),

which add another chromatic half-tone to the already raised or lowered basic tone.

Thus we obtain the following tritones and diminished fifths:

(2) The restoration of a basic tone after its doubly raised or lowered form is done by a *single* natural:

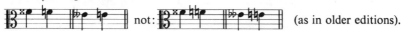 (as in older editions).

The single chromatic alteration of a tone after a × or ♭♭ should be marked by a ♯ or ♭ solely:

—— EXERCISE 48 ——

1. Play the following tones; sing the tones a tritone (or diminished fifth) above the upper tones:

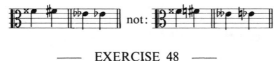

2. Invent similar examples.
3. Play; sing the tones a tritone or diminished fifth below the lowest tones:

4. Invent similar examples.

[145]

NOTATION: The use of $\times$ and $\flat\flat$ permits the construction of some additional major scales, such as G♯, D♯, F♭.

—— EXERCISE 49 ——

Write these three major scales in alto clef through two octaves.

NOTATION: (1) These scales are but other forms (*enharmonic* transcriptions) of simpler scales already known, namely those on A♭, E♭, and E. Without urgent reason no one is likely to write a scale with six sharps and one double sharp if he can obtain the same result with merely four flats. Sometimes, however, the harmonic context of a piece compels us to use the more complicated notation. Thus a temporary modulation in E major to the major key on the third degree has to be written in G♯ major and not in A♭ major, since the intermixture of numerous flats and sharps, and even the rapid change from one group of accidentals to the other is as far as possible to be avoided.

(2) In the major scales originally constructed (6 with sharps, 6 with flats, 1 without accidentals—see Chapters V and VI) we already relied on one enharmonic transcription: the scales on F♯ and G♭ are identical in sound but different in notation. One has the key-signature of 6 sharps, the other of 6 flats. This leads us to a rule:

The sharps and flats in the signatures of enharmonically equivalent scales always add up to a total of 12 accidentals.

Thus: the key-signature of A♭ major is 4 flats, and that of its enharmonic equivalent G♯ major would be 8 sharps—6 normal sharps and 1 double sharp. But in practice, while keys containing more than 7 sharps or flats are occasionally used (as a result of modulations in the course of pieces in simpler keys), they are never indicated in signatures.

—— EXERCISE 50 ——

Write the major scales on C♭ and C♯, in alto clef.

Question: What are the key-signatures of these scales?

If we arrange all the major scales, starting with C, progressing according to the number of their sharps in one direction and of their flats in the other, we see that they follow each other at the distance of a fifth and a fourth respectively.

The one series is called the *circle of fifths*, the other the *circle of fourths*. In both there is a region where enharmonic transcription provides two forms of several scales:

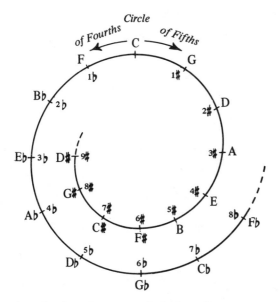

On the piano both series are real circles: they return to their starting point.

This is not true in natural (non-tempered) tuning. Here the circle is replaced by a spiral, and the twelfth fifth reaches a point which (after some octave transpositions) is slightly sharper than the starting point, while the twelfth fourth produces a tone which is correspondingly too flat. The mass of enharmonic complexity in notation gives us an approximate idea of the extent to which this tonal overgrowth accumulates.

It would be quite impossible to keep order and consistency in musical procedures if the singers and the players of untempered instruments did not unconsciously find their way back to a simpler tonal context. This highly complicated mental process, with its innumerable gradations of shifts and tone-adaptions, can at least be schematically understood by a glimpse at the preceding figure: whenever one proceeds too far into the flats or sharps one can always shift over to the next parallel track of the spiral, so as to get back into regions of less complicated tonal relationship.

Enharmonic transcription makes possible the construction of diminished and augmented derivations of each perfect, major, or minor interval.

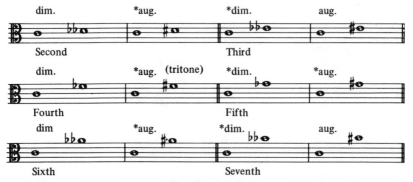

dim.   *aug.   *dim.   aug.

Second   Third

dim.   *aug. (tritone)   *dim.   *aug.

Fourth   Fifth

dim   *aug.   *dim.   aug.

Sixth   Seventh

Those marked * occur rather frequently in certain harmonic constellations; the others are rarely used.

The inversion of an augmented interval is always diminished, and vice versa:

Even the octave can appear in a diminished or augmented form,

and, in analogy to the other intervals, the same ought to be true for its inversion, the *Prime (Unison)*. Here, however, we encounter several obstacles. First: our musical feeling hesitates to acknowledge different forms of something that owing to its definition (*unison*) can have only one. Moreover: the inversion of a diminished octave is an augmented prime, so the inversion of an augmented octave would be a diminished prime:

Here again it is rather unconvincing to define (in contradiction of all other interval definitions) the flattened form of the prime as augmented and the sharpened one as diminished. The most practical correction of this oddity is simply to name the chromatic half-step formed by a tone and its chromatic alteration an *augmented prime* (c—c♯, c—c♭, c♭—c♮, c♯—c♮).

Like the tritone and the diminished fifth all other augmented and diminished intervals have the tendency to lean towards other, stronger intervals. In a context devoid of accidentals or one in which sharps prevail, flats (or ♭♭) generally indicate a downward melodic tendency; the converse is also true.

NOTATION: All these intervals are, as far as sound is concerned, only written variations of the simpler basic (perfect, major, and minor) intervals, at least on the piano: the keyboard makes no distinction between an augmented second and a minor third. That despite this simple fact we so often use the more complicated forms of "spelling" instead of their undiminished and unaugmented equivalents, is again due to the ambiguous character of our notation. In notation we try as far as possible to express the melodic and harmonic functions of tones and intervals.

For instance, the relationship tonic-dominant is written without exception as a perfect fifth and not as a diminished sixth; and the interval from the leading tone to the tonic will always be a minor second and not an augmented prime. Half-tone steps leading into main functional tones (tonic, dominant, subdominant, leading tone), must generally be written as diatonic half-tones (provided the harmonic context demands no other orthography), and it is obvious that with all these and similar regulations and restrictions the notation of augmented and diminished intervals is inevitable.

—— EXERCISE 51 ——

1. Name the following intervals:

   e♭—f♯, d—b♯, b—a♭', g♭—b♭♭, c♯—c♮, c♯—d♭, c♯—c×, a—c♭', b♯—g', a♯—a', d♯—g, e♯—e×', a—c♭', f♯—e', g♯—d♯', e♭—b, a♭♭—d♭'.

2. Name the following tones:

   (a) Augmented primes of f, b♯, a♭, e×, g♭♭;
   (b) the diminished second above b, d, g♯ a×;
   (c) the augmented second above f♯, c♭, d♭♭, b;
   (d) the diminished third above d♯, a×, d, g;
   (e) the augmented third above b, f♭, c♯, a♭♭;
   (f) the diminished fourth above a, d×, b♯, c♭;
   (g) the augmented fourth above e♭♭, b♯, f♭, c♭♭;
   (h) the diminished fifth above g♭, e♯, d×, f♭;
   (i) the augmented fifth above e, a♭♭, b, c♭;
   (j) the diminished sixth above f♯, e×, g, b♭;
   (k) the augmented sixth above e, c♭, g♭♭, a;
   (l) the diminished seventh above d, a♭, e♯, f×;
   (m) the augmented seventh above f♭, g, b♭♭, e;
   (n) the diminished octave above c×, b♭, e♯, a;
   (o) the augmented octave above f♭, d♯, g♭♭, b.

[149]

3. What intervals are these?

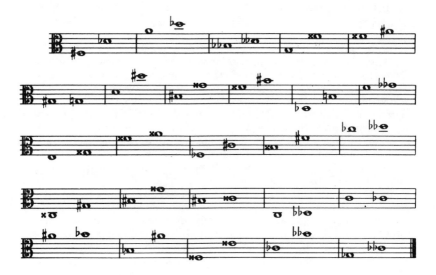

4. Play given tones or chords on the piano and sing tone-progressions involving diminished and augmented intervals (one octave lower for men's voices).

(a) Sing the progression: aug. 2nd—maj. 3rd above the upper tone:

Model:

(b) Sing aug. 5th—maj. 6th above the upper tone:

Model:

(c) Sing dim. 7th—min. 6th above the upper tone:

Model.

(d) Sing the following progressions above the upper tone: dim. 5th—dim. 4th—dim. 3rd, and end in unison with the upper tone of the second chord:

Model:

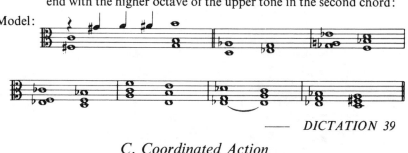

(e) Sing in the same manner: aug. 5th—maj. 6th—aug. 6th, and end with the higher octave of the upper tone in the second chord:

Model:

—— *DICTATION 39*

C. Coordinated Action

—— EXERCISE 52 ——

1. Play on the piano, adding the accidentals for the key marked at the beginning of each piece. You may, if you want, add other obstacles, of the kind provided in Exercise 44, paragraph 1.

Moderato in G♯ major

(e)

2. Sing; beat time:

Allegro

(a)

Moderato

(b)

NOTATION: (1) The degrees of loudness are indicated by

$f = forte$

$p = piano$

and their augmented and reduced forms:

ff (*fortissimo*), fff

pp (*pianissimo*), ppp

mf (*mezzo forte*) = *softer* than forte

mp (*mezzo piano*) = *louder* than piano.

"*più*" and "*meno*" are also used in combination with f and p.

The symbol fp represents a kind of dynamic accent (*forte*, and immediately *piano*); similar effects are indicated by:

sf, sfz, fz (*sforzato* or *sforzando*) = forcing, pressing, i.e., suddenly stressed.

(2) The gradual change from one degree of loudness to another is marked:

cresc. (*crescendo*), or: ———

dim. (*diminuendo*), or: *decrescendo*, or: ————

the gradation being sometimes emphasized by an added "*poco a poco*."

The symbols for loudness are the same in all languages.

(3) Besides the terms for tempo and degrees of loudness, composers use a great number of other explanatory terms in order to give— as far as possible— a more minute description of the mood and character to be expressed in performing their music. In fact the entire arsenal of those adjectives and participles which are related to tempo, mood, and dynamics can be used. Therefore it would be a bold enterprise to attempt to give in the realm of this book an even superficial outline of the possibilities. The reader must rely on a special dictionary of musical terms.

There are, however, certain standard terms, used everywhere, some of which may follow here:

affettuoso—innig—affectueux = tender, expressive;

agitato—lebhaft bewegt—agité = agitated;

amabile—lieblich—aimable = amiable;

con anima—munter—avec verve = with spirit;

animato—belebt—animé = spirited;

appassionato—leidenschaftlich—passionné = impassioned;

arioso = singing;

con brio—schwungvoll—avec verve = with dash, with fire;

cantabile—gesangvoll—chantant = singing;

dolce—zart—doucement, doux = sweet;

dolente—klagend—triste = grieving;

con dolore—schmerzlich, kummervoll—douloureux = with grief;

con fuoco = feurig—ardent = with fire;

giocoso—scherzhaft—en badinant = playfully;

gioioso—freudig—joyeux = joyously;

grazioso—zierlich—gracieux = gracefully;

leggiero—leicht—léger = lightly;

lusingando—schmeichelnd—caressant = caressingly;

maestoso—feierlich, würdig—majestueux = majestically;

marziale—kriegerisch = martially;

misterioso—geheimnisvoll—mystérieux = mysteriously;

con moto = bewegt—mouvementé = with movement;

perdendosi—verlöschend—en s'effaçant = disappearing;

[155]

piacevole—gefällig—plaisant = smoothly, agreeably;
risoluto—entschlossen—résolu = resolutely;
scherzando—scherzend = jokingly;
sostenuto—getragen—soutenu = sustained;
teneramente—zärtlich—tendre = tenderly;
tenuto—gehalten—tenu = held.

Hand in hand with these terms go hundreds of others designating musical forms and customs, others referring to historical developments, still others giving instrumental and vocal, orchestral and choral directions—and so forth. In the realm of our present work the mere mentioning of this fact must suffice. Again a good dictionary and additional studies are recommended for those who want to be regarded as well-educated musicians.

CHAPTER XI

A. Action in Time

While music theory has discovered the basic principles of melody and harmony, it has not yet been able to find satisfactory explanations for those higher constructive functions of meter and rhythm that make up what is generally known as "*Musical Form*". We know empirically how to build forms, and by analysing existing compositions we can arrive at certain rules of thumb for form-construction. But the underlying laws upon which such construction is based are still a secret to musicians, at least as far as conscious understanding and formulation are concerned. What is usually taught in schools as "form" is only the analytic process of taking apart pre-constructed forms, and has nothing in common with the creative process of building up such forms—a synthesis based on laws more fundamental than the mere regulations derived from practical experience, or from copying older works.

Hence it is not possible to provide within the framework of this book exercises which would enable the student to reproduce and practise patterns of form as he has reproduced and practised patterns of rhythm (meter), harmony, and melody. But in order to give at least some information about musical form, although only in rudiments and as a stimulus to the student's own thinking rather than as a ready-made explanation, a short survey of some materials for a possible theory of form follows.

A musical form is a temporal entity, of which, as of any temporal entity in other artistic activities (poem, drama, lecture, film, etc.), the aesthetic effect as a whole cannot be comprehended until it reaches a conclusion in a final tone or chord. Thus judgment of the aesthetic effect or technical shape of a temporal form is necessarily retrospective. Nothing can be added or subtracted in the course of the unfolding of such a form (not even single tones) without destroying the form and replacing it by a new one.

In analysis, the entity can, of course, be split up into its smallest particles: we can trace the formal functions down to the minutest metric units, two-beat or three-beat groups (see Chapter VIII), and to the basic rhythmic grouping of a "motive" (a term for which there is no exact definition generally agreed upon by theorists). But any rhythmic or metric section longer than these smallest units has an effect upon us quite different from the mere accumulation of the effects of smaller constituent parts. Although the position and function of each constituent part is determined by the higher requirements of the entity, and although this entity cannot exist without the accumulated effects of its constituents, yet as a completed temporal form it creates effects of a higher and independent aesthetic order.

Thus we see that the casual relationship between the work of art and its aesthetic effect has no connection with the laws of simple arithmetic. The smallest metric and rhythmic units, previously mentioned, are therefore only the ultimate subdivisions and ramifications of the powerful metric and rhythmic pulsations that organize the general temporal outlines of a musical form and divide it into movements and sections, peaks and valleys of intensity, and so on down to the very smallest subordinate units.

This higher metric-and-rhythmic (formal) power influences the two other constructive elements, melody and harmony, and is in turn influenced in its own course by them. Subordinate musical elements such as dynamics, tone-color, phrasing, etc., may also influence the aural impression of a musical form, but they cannot modify its construction, since their power is merely decorative, not constructive.

The effects of formal construction embodied in rhythm, melody, and harmony are compound, being achieved through various factors:

(a) Duration, which can be measured by a clock.
(b) Tempo (uniform or changing), which can be measured by a metronome.
(c) Relative speed of unfolding (proportional inter-relationships of the constituent parts), for which we do not know what means of measurement to use.
(d) Closeness (degree of complexity) of texture, for which, also, we possess no means of measurement.

The principles by which the compound effects are achieved when the sounding material is cast into molds of temporal construction are three:

(a) Repetition (re-use of one constituent part of the formal entity, on the same pitch level, or in transposition).
(b) Variation (some of the elements of a constituent part are changed while others remain unchanged. For instance, the melodic line may be retained but with different harmonic and rhythmic treatment; or the rhythmic shape of a motive—or melody, etc.—may be retained, but with changed melodic outline and new harmonies).

Between the literal repetition of a given material and complete change to new material there are infinite gradations, their complexity increased by the inclusion of the aforementioned subordinate, decorative elements. It is in the application of the principle of variation that a composer's power and intelligence in formal construction manifests itself most obviously.

(c) Change (one constituent part gives place to an entirely different one).

In constructing a musical form— either by recreating a form used in the past or by building up a new one on a strictly theoretical basis—the emphasis at any given moment may be on any one of the aforementioned factors, or on more than one of them. Not only do different musical forms vary widely in their treatment of these factors, but even in one and the same form-category the means of expression vary with different periods, individualities, technical and sociological conditions of performance, etc. The same composer, even in two pieces belonging to the same form-category, will never use the constructive factors in exactly the same way. His is an infinite number of possibilities in calculating the dimensions and choosing permutations and combinations for his building stones. In this procedure, he is guided by the accumulated experience of previous composers, and by considerations generally covered by such vague terms as talent, inspiration, purpose, taste, etc. But obviously even the most independent and most radically inspired talent, irrespective of taste and purpose, must, in the construction of his musical forms, follow a pathway the landmarks of which are immovably fixed by nature.

It is the task of a future theory of music to discover and formulate the laws of form, which will introduce into the realms of the higher functions of meter and rhythm the same order and thorough organization we already enjoy in the fields of harmonic and melodic construction.

B. Action in Space

NOTATION: (1) Besides the alto clef another c'-clef is used for the middle region of our tone system: the *Tenor Clef*.

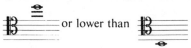

Although it was formerly used in writing for the high male voice and its instrumental equivalents, it is nowadays used only for the higher regions of 'Cello, Bassoon, and Trombone (sometimes even Double Bass). Ledger lines are rarely written higher than

or lower than

(2) In writing vocal music, a tendency towards using hybrid clefs for the

tenor region is spreading nowadays. They are and similar forms, invariably transposing the notes of the treble clef one octave lower. An excuse for the introduction of these rather amateurish inventions may be found in the modern neglect of proficiency in clef-reading and transposing, in which neglect singers usually even surpass other categories of musicians. For a musician of some culture it is always contemptible to rely on such stop-gaps, not because it is praiseworthy to overcome difficult obstacles when there is an easier way to approach a goal, and not out of mere traditional prejudices, but because it is absurd musical provincialism not to understand the complete range of musical tones as a whole (out of which we may cut any section and place it in any conceivable way upon the staff lines), instead of having to rely, for lack of experience in the craft of the musician, on one or two standard clefs in order to write and read any given tone.

(3) The now obsolete c'-clefs on the first and second staff-lines (soprano and mezzo-soprano clef respectively) are for advanced students of the same importance as alto and tenor clefs, since most of the pre-Classic music uses them. Perfect ability to read them fluently (singly and in combinations) is essential! The same is true (though in a lesser degree) for other f- and g'-clefs, such as:

—— EXERCISE 53 ——

1. Name the following notes:

2. Play on the piano:

Intervals exceeding the octave use as names the ordinal numbers ninth, tenth, etc., although they are in fact but repetitions of the intervals within the octave. Thus: ninth = second, tenth = third, eleventh = fourth, twelfth = fifth.

Still larger intervals are named as combinations of the octave and the interval exceeding it, such as octave and sixth, octave and seventh, up to and exceeding the double octave.

In certain very complex harmonic progressions now and then doubly diminished or doubly augmented intervals may occur. It is needless to prove again that they are caused merely by the ambiguity of notation, and that in sound they are identical with simpler intervals or deviate only slightly from them (see page 144 ff).

—— EXERCISE 54 ——

1. Name the following intervals:

[161]

2. Write a number of doubly augmented and doubly diminished intervals on different notes.

—— *DICTATION 42*

The freedom in handling intervals gained in the last chapters now permits us the construction of the *Minor Scale*, in music theory the second handy array of diatonic material used in composition since about 1600.

In the minor scale certain features are the same as in the major; in others it differs from its simpler prototype.

Both have in common: the tonic, the second degree (sometimes called the *Supertonic*), the subdominant, and the dominant.

Entirely different is the third degree. In minor it is the minor third of the tonic, a half-tone above the second degree (*e*-flat in *c* minor).

NOTATION: In theoretical work all names of minor keys are written with small letters, in contrast to the capitals used to designate major (*see page 54*).

The sixth and seventh degrees in minor are variable: sometimes they correspond with those in major (major 6th, major 7th), in other cases minor 6th and minor 7th are used, or minor 6th and major 7th.

The total supply of tones contained in the major and various forms of minor scales on *c* is, accordingly, as follows:

Major:

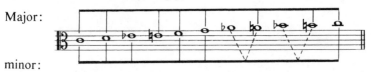

minor:

The variability of the sixth and seventh degrees permits the following combinations for the upper part of the minor scale:

Number 1 is used in the *melodic* minor scale, but only upwards; downwards, number 4 replaces it. Thus:

in C

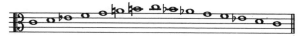

Number 2 upwards *and* downwards is the *harmonic* minor scale. Note the characteristic step of this scale: the augmented 2nd between the sixth and seventh degrees:

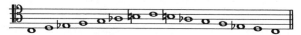

Number 3 is an obsolete form, identical with the *Church Mode:* Dorian*.

Number 4 is the so-called *natural* minor scale.

Numbers 3 and 4 are regarded as less important, because they lack one of the main functional tones (leading tone), which occurs in the harmonic form in both directions, and in the melodic form at least upwards.

*The church modes are scales based primarily on melodic considerations; they preceded, and for the most part were replaced by, our major and minor scales, which are better adapted to harmonic purposes. There is an older form, which represents the entire tone material of the vocal, unaccompanied ritual music of the Roman Catholic church (Gregorian chant), in use since early in the Christian era and up until to-day.

It consisted of seven tones, corresponding generally with our seven scale tones *c d e f g a b*, which could however, be placed on any pitch within the range of the human voice. Any tone could be "*c*," provided the other tones were arranged, as regards the position of the half-tone steps, according to the original model (an unconscious "transposition," as we should say). Their names were the six syllables Ut Re Mi Fa Sol La, used singly or in combinations (*c* = fa ut, *a* = la mi re, *c'* = sol fa ut); later (16th century) a seventh syllable—Si, corresponding with our *b*—was added.

These tones were the building material for eight seven-tone scales (modes), which were grouped into pairs by common *finals* (ending tones = tonics). Thus Modes I and II were built on what we, by intentional anachronism, call "*d*" (solre, re),

III and IV on "*e*",
V and VI on "*f*",
VII and VIII on "*g*".

[163]

Number 4, however, determines the key-signature of the minor tonality, which is the same as that of the major scale one minor 3rd higher, called the *relative* major. This means that the raised leading tone in minor is never shown in the key-signature, but always has to be marked wherever it appears on the staff line. The same is true for the raised sixth degree (as in scale No. 1). Thus: *f♯* minor has the same key-signature as *A* major, but its *e♯* (and *d♯*) are not marked at the beginning of the staff line.

—— EXERCISE 55 ——

Name the relative minor or major scales of:

A, D♭, g, E, b, B, a♭, C♯, c♯ G♭, d♯, B♭, a,
D, d, F, f♯, c, E♭, e♭, F♯, g♯, b♭, e, G, C, f.

How many sharps or flats do their key-signatures have?

The aforementioned distance of a minor scale from a major scale with the same number of accidentals gives us a clue to the construction of the circles of fifths and fourths respectively for minor scales.

—— EXERCISE 56 ——

Name (a) the circle of fifths starting with *a* minor and going up to seven sharps;

(b) the circle of fourths starting with *a* minor, going up to eight flats.

The *ambitus* (approximate ranges) of the two scales having the same finals were different, however:

I (or Dorian) starts on *d*,
II (or Hypodorian) starts on *a*,
III (or Phrygian) starts on *e*,
IV (or Hypophrygian) starts on *b*,
V (or Lydian) starts on *f*,
VI (or Hypolydian) starts on *c*,
VII (or Mixolydian) starts on *g*,
VIII (or Hypomixolydian) starts again on *d*.

Melodies in these modes, although they may liberally exceed the compass of an octave, move mainly between the final and the *repercussa* (tenor, dominant, recitation-tone) of each. The repercussae are:

a in I,   *f* in II,   *c* in III,   *a* in IV,
c in V,   *a* in VI,   *d* in VII,   *c* in VIII.

The attempt to accommodate the church modes to the demands of harmonic writing

C. Coordinated Action

—— EXERCISE 57 ——

1. Sing, as described in Exercise 20, in succession the melodic, harmonic, Dorian, and natural (Aeolian) forms of minor scales.

(a) in *c*, *g*, *b♭*, *f*:

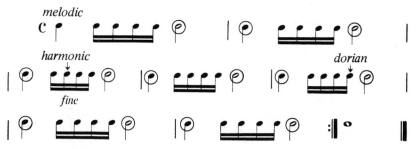

The repetition starts with the natural scale.

(b) in *e*, *f♯*, *d*, *a:*

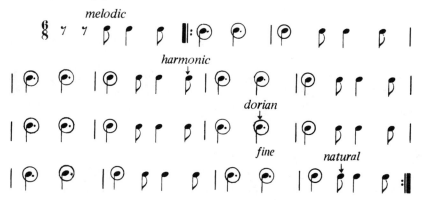

---

led to a revised system as immediate predecessor of our major and minor scales. This system is still in use in the old-fashioned method of school counterpoint. It differs from the original system by its fixed dominants in its modes (a fifth distant from the final); furthermore triads (major or minor) can be built on each tonic, and each fourth and fifth degree. The scale-names in this system are Dorian (on *d*), Phrygian (on *e*), Lydian (on *f*), Mixolydian (on *g*), Aeolian (on *a*), and Ionian (on *c*). Aeolian corresponds with our minor scale number 4, Ionian with the major scale; in Dorian and Phrygian we find close approximations to minor, in Lydian and Mixolydian to major.

[165]

(c) in e♭, c♯, g♯, d♭:

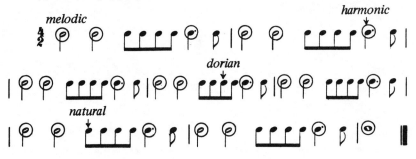

(d) in d♯, a♭, b, a♯:

2. Play a chord on the piano. Sing the c minor scale, upwards and down-wards in its melodic and harmonic forms. The procedure is as described in Exercise 38, paragraph 3. For men's voices: Play one octave higher, sing one octave lower.

Chords to be played:

3. Play on the piano. While playing add the accidentals necessary for the key marked at the beginning of each piece. The accidentals for the sixth and seventh degrees are already marked.

Allegro assai in e♭ minor

(a)

Allegro in c♯ minor

(b)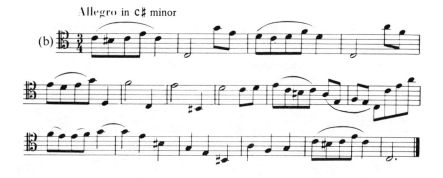

Allegretto scherzando in e minor

(c)

[167]

Notation: Although not used in the elementary exercises of this book, certain peculiarities of notation may be mentioned here.

(a) *Abbreviations*. For the repetition of notes, figures, and measures, short-hand symbols are sometimes used, which, with the knowledge gained so far, ought to be self-explanatory.

Written form:

To be played:

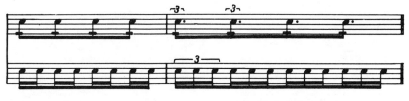

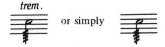

Written form:	To be played:

Written form:

trem.

 or simply

To be played:

Repetition of the same tone, as fast as possible, without a distinct rhythm (*tremolo*).

Adagio

Tremolo legato. Fast repetition of two alternating tones at the distance of at least a minor third.

In slow tempo the three or more beams put between the two notes may mean a definite rhythmical undulation of $\frac{1}{32}$ or $\frac{1}{64}$ time-values. In order to secure a genuine tremolo without definitely recognizable regular alternation of the two tones, the addition of the word *trem.* is necessary.

In writing *tremolo legato* both notes of a group are given the metric value that the group as a whole has. In groups that count a quarter or less, the beams must not touch the stems; with half-notes two kinds of writing are permissible. Thus:

Alternating notes connected by only one or two tremolo beams can always be regarded as figures consisting of regular $\frac{1}{8}$ or $\frac{1}{16}$ notes:

This latter kind of notation is also used for *non legato* execution (without slurs).

[169]

Written form:	*To be played:*
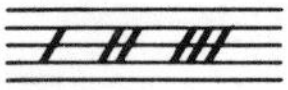	Repeat the last beamed group of eighths, sixteenths, or thirty-seconds, respectively.
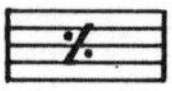	Repeat the preceding measure.
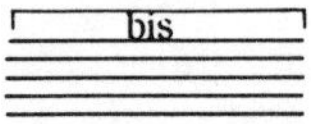	Repeat everything under the bracket.

(b) *Rests longer than one measure* are written thus:

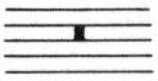 = two measures, 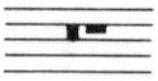 = three measures, 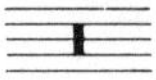 = 4 mm.,

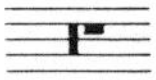 = 5 mm., 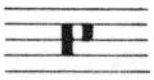 = 6 mm., 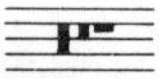 = 7 mm., 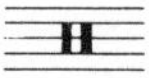 = 8 mm.

Mostly a number is added to facilitate reading:

Rests exceeding eight measures are written thus: 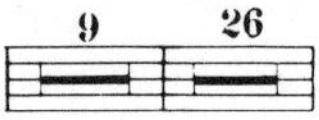

(c) *Ornaments.* Of the tremendous variety of abbreviations for ornamental figures once in use (especially during the 18th century*) only a few are still alive. Nowadays the prevalent tendency is to write out each ornament, and so avoid all ambiguity.

In performing *grace-notes* the general agreement is that they are fractional parts of the main notes with which they are connected by slurs. Thus the following grace-notes:

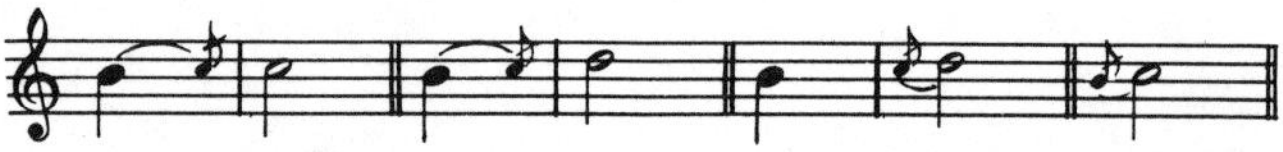

are to be played:

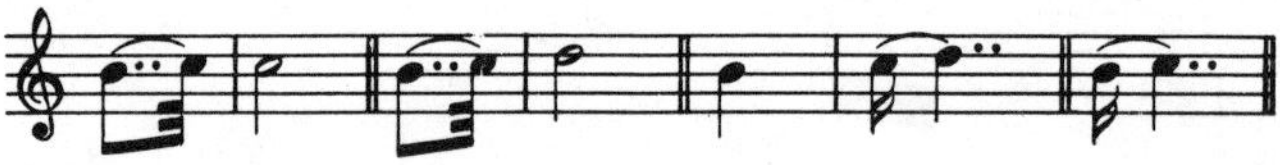

and not:

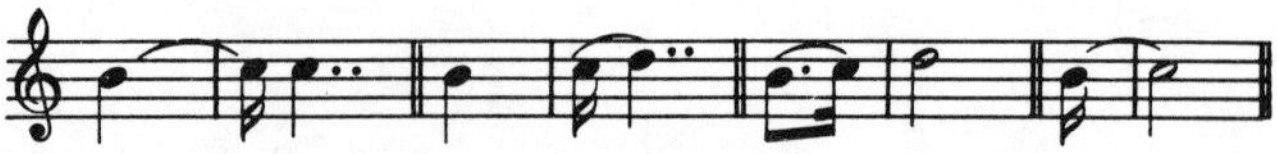

The *trill* is a legato tremolo with the upper neighbor of a tone:

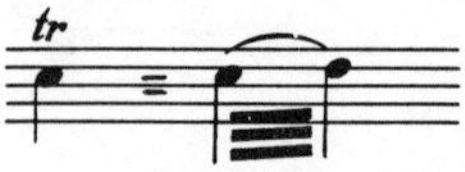

On very short notes it can include only one appearance of the upper tone. A trill may begin with the main tone or with its upper neighbor, the latter form being more frequently used.

*See special explanations in editions of 18th-century music.

The habit of ending a trill with one or two grace-notes

is so inveterate that these endings need not be written; on the contrary: a special remark is necessary for a trill without concluding grace-note, except in the case of a tied-over trill:

Andante

In the rare instances when a trill uses the lower neighbor of the main note, it must be written as a tremolo legato:

In keyboard music (in rare cases in music for stringed instruments) the

sign

stands for the harp-like effect of *arpeggio* (or *arpeggiando*):

Nowadays completely out of use is the *long grace-note*, which in spite of its miniature size was generally played like a full-sized note of the same order:

Almost completely obsolete are the *Pralltriller* and the *Mordent:*

also the *turn*, either on one single note, or between two notes:

In the latter case it is generally executed on the second half (in fast tempo) or the last fourth (slow) of the first note when the latter is bipartite, or on the last third or sixth when it is tripartite:

[171]

A certain ambiguity prevails, however, concerning the use of turns. Sometimes a distinction is made between ∾ (starting with the upper neighboring tone) and its counterpart ∾ , and some musicians hold that a turn added to a dotted note must be played so that the value represented by the dot sounds in its full length:

(d) *Articulation*. The slur as symbol of articulation demands a *legato* execution (see page 37). The opposite effect (*staccato*) is symbolized by dots or "wedges" above or below the heads of the notes. Notes with such additions are to be sung or played with a shorter metric value than indicated, followed by a rest:

The wedge is generally regarded as a sign for intensification of the staccato:

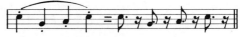

Dots within a slur imply:
  in keyboard notation, a "portato" execution:

and for string instruments, the playing of a number of short staccato tones on a single stroke of the bow, either downwards (⊓) or upwards (∨).
  A slight lengthening of a tone is demanded by a dash, or by the word *ten.* (= tenuto):

—— EXERCISE 58 ——

1. Sing, beat time. Additional obstacles as in Exercise 44. Name the key. Women's voices sing one octave higher.

Sing ½ tone lower.

Allegretto grazioso

(b)

$\flat = \flat.$ *of preceding*

Andante espressivo

Sing ½ tone higher.

(c)

Sing in *g* and in *a*.

[173]

In singing these two transposed forms you will observe that to a certain degree real transposition can be replaced by clef-transposition: the transposition of this piece to *g* can be achieved by reading the original in treble clef, and the notes read in alto clef give you the transposition to *a*. But you will soon find out the weakness of this procedure! Real transposition transfers each interval of the original to its new place in its exact size, while in clef-transposition the fixed half-tones *e—f* and *b—c* of the clef frequently appear in places where the original has whole-tone steps. Hence it is not advisable to rely in transposition on clef-reading. The safe way is to take in as quickly as possible the tonal structure in the original key with all its intervals, and transfer it as a whole to the new tonic. Only by frequently practising this method (not by transposing merely the few pieces in this book!) can you acquire perfect fluency and accuracy in transposition.

Sing in *g♯* and *f*.

Major and minor scales, in spite of their usefulness and the fact that they are sanctioned by tradition and habit, have one great disadvantage: they are, like all other kinds of diatonic scales, already "composed" structures. Melodies following their patterns must necessarily be limited by the already melodic distribution of the raw material, and harmonic progressions built upon their measurements cannot transgress certain confines of tonal construction without bringing the entire system of diatonic tonality to the verge of chaos.

Hence music theory in recent decades has shown a strong trend towards the use of a more neutral scale material, which has all the advantages of the diatonic major and minor scales without sharing their limitations.

We can get an approximate idea of such an extended tonal material when we imagine that the free use of tones, as observed in the upper half of our minor scale, can be applied throughout the whole octave, thus providing abundant material for melodic as well as harmonic purposes.

The *chromatic scale* is the simplest and most obvious display of this richer material. It consists of twelve half-tones to the octave, but in spite of the equal distance of its tones the main tonal functions (tonic, dominants, leading tone) remain with the same tones as in major and minor. Thus in the chromatic scale on *c* the main functional tones are, as ever, *c*, *f*, *g*, and *b*.

This is not the place to develop theories of the chromatic scale, nor can we enlarge upon discussions concerning the technical possibilities and aesthetic qualities of chromaticism. Certain rules about its handling in notation and some practical examples may, however, be given.

NOTATION: Although the urge upwards in a scale implies in general the use of sharps for chromatically altered tones (see p. 149), and the reverse impulse demands flats, the notation of chromaticism is above all determined by the harmonic function of the tones: as long as the chromatically altered notes are parts of the simpler intervals (fifth, fourth, the two thirds, and the two sixths) they have to be written as such and not as their enharmonic equivalents (as already stated; see the discussion following Exercise 49).

Sometimes, however, the *melodic* function of a tone has the first claim to expression in notation (for instance, in the diatonic step *leading-tone to tonic*); then it is simply not possible to satisfy equally the notational demands of both kinds of functions.

If there are no obvious harmonic implications—as in the case of an unaccompanied chromatic scale—we generally follow the upward or downward tendency of the accidentals. Owing to the inherent harmonic strength of dominant and subdominant, however, the tones representing these functions are always written as the fifth and fourth of the tonic, both upwards and downwards. Furthermore the minor seventh of the tonic is usually written as such in both directions, and not as an augmented sixth preceding and preparing the leading-tone. For the half-tone between dominant and subdominant there is no set rule in downward notation.

[175]

—— EXERCISE 59 ——

1. Write chromatic scales on *e*, *b*♭, *f*♯, *c*♭ etc., in tenor clef.
2. Sing, beating time:

Fine

D.C. al Fine

Part Two

DICTATION

PREFACE TO PART TWO

Dictation, as it appears in the curricula of our music schools, namely as a separate course, unrelated to other more important subjects, is in my opinion an almost completely useless part of musical education. Sometimes excellent musicians are not able to write down even comparatively simple dictated examples, while frequently musicians of inferior quality easily reproduce elaborate dictations. This shows that the ability to follow musical dictation is not necessarily an index of the degree or quality of musical talent, any more than the memory for numbers, the gift to imitate others' actions, or the sense for spatial direction are essential criteria for general intelligence.

On the other hand it cannot be denied that the complete absence of such ability is at least an unfavourable indication of the state of a musician's knowledge. It is therefore necessary to develop it—whatever its amount or quality may be—to the utmost, just as all other parts of his gift must be developed. (This by no means warrants a separate dictation course, stretched out over a whole year or even longer!) To meet this necessity, the most reasonable way of using dictation is to combine it with other musical activities and apply it merely to check up on the general development. The understanding of rhythmic phrases, harmonic progressions, and melodic lines can easily be re-checked by dictating similar material. Not only is this one of the few ways a teacher can follow the student's methods of tackling and solving problems, but such combined activity also makes palatable a course otherwise essentially dry, unpleasant, and boring.

These statements ought to make clear what the purpose of the following exercises is: they follow closely the examples given in the first part of the book, each one using the material that has been worked out in the actively performed example which precedes it. There is no doubt that any student who has mastered the material in its first form must be able to write down its dictated equivalent; he will thus improve his dictation work along with his progress in reading, singing, and playing.

More than in the first part of the book the teacher must here use his own judgement as to how the exercises ought to be applied. He will find that there is no uniformity of reactions to a dictated example. Each individuality in a class has its own tempo and method of approach. But

[181]

in spite of this great variety there are only two essentially different methods. They are the two ways listeners follow in perceiving and understanding music in general. One group catches primarily the general impression of a musical structure, and through further analytical thinking—with the aid of repeated apperceptions of the same material or of conclusions based on memory and logic—discovers and adds the constituent parts, thus literally filling out the pre-established musical form.

Of no less importance is the other method, which adds up great numbers of single aural impressions, till in the listener's mind the complete form is synthetically reconstructed.

A well experienced musician will never rely on either of these two methods alone but will always mix them, using at any given moment (consciously or intuitively) the one that gives him the greater push forward.

In dictating the exercises the teacher must take into account both methods of approach. He must know which of them he wants to emphasize with each example, and he must inform the class of his intentions.

The students' abilities to perceive primarily the general outlines of an example will be promoted by dictating in fast tempo, and by frequent repetitions of a complete example. In dictating melodic lines it is advisable to let the students symbolize their course graphically in a continuous pencil line, before writing them down in notes. After the first vague impression has settled, main points of the example may be fixed, such as the beginning and ending, climaxes, prominent tones or rhythms, and then the remaining parts must be filled in. With growing experience the number of repeated playings necessary for the complete result will gradually decrease.

Fast playing with few repetitions (the number of repetitions should be announced in advance) serves as a test for the increasing speed of apperception. From a fixed number of, say, five playings, a student may at first gain nothing but a very vague impression of the examples, and he may only later become able to grasp most of their contents in this number of hearings.

Frequent interspersed questions about names of certain tones, values of notes, etc., may be used to sharpen the students' attentive faculty.

To develop the second, detailed method of hearing, it is recommended that the examples be split up at first into smaller sections (bars, motives); moreover, in exercises for coordinated action, the rhythmic structure may at first be dictated separately from the melodic line, until the students are able to grasp both together. Here also the emphasis can always be shifted from accuracy to speed by modifying the tempo of dictation as well as the number of repetitions.

In addition, the students should use the blackboard, constantly watched and corrected by their fellow students, and they should take turns at substituting for the teacher in singing or playing the material which the other students are to write from their dictation. These and other variations will add life and richness to the dictation part of the present method, and will most effectively further the students' all-round musicianship.

Although the teacher must insist on strictest accuracy in both the contents of the reproduced dictated examples and their graphic appearance, he ought to be rather lenient in one respect: he should not mark as mistakes minor deviations from his dictated model if they are merely different interpretations of an aural impression. Thus frequently a dotted note may appear on the student's work sheet as a note with a rest instead of the augmentation dot; beams may be used instead of flags or hooks, and vice versa; and even ambiguous "spelling" may occasionally be permissible.

In all dictation courses the main danger is that they very easily degenerate into a kind of quiz. Nothing is so senseless as to combine musical aims with the idea of mental competition or even with a mere childish sort of riddle-guessing. The higher a teacher can maintain the musical level of his classes' dictation exercises the better he will serve their artistic purpose.

CHAPTER I

DICTATION 1 ——

TEACHER: Tap the beats and sing a tone where brackets are marked.
PUPIL: Mark on a sheet of paper or on the blackboard 8 short vertical dashes (for beats). Mark with brackets the tones you hear sung.

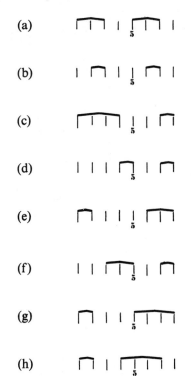

Add similar exercises, if necessary.

DICTATION 2 ——

TEACHER: Tap the beats and play tones where notes are marked.
PUPIL: Mark 10 beats on paper or on the blackboard. Write notes for
the tones you hear played.

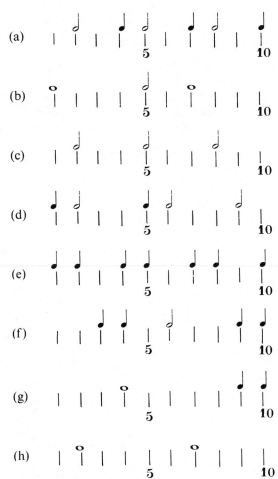

Add similar exercises, if necessary.

DICTATION 3 ——

(1) TEACHER: Tap the beats and sing tones where notes are marked.
   PUPIL: Listen. At the repetition sing tones where the teacher has
   rests.

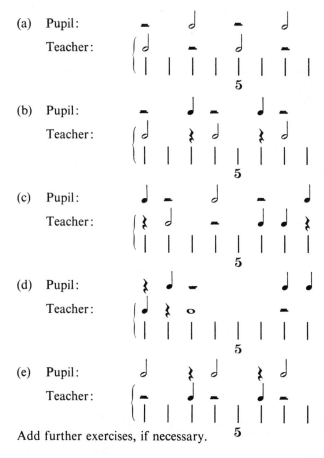

Add further exercises, if necessary.

(2) TEACHER: Tap the beats and play a tone where notes are marked.
PUPIL: Mark 10 beats on paper or on the blackboard. Listen. Write
rests above your beats when the teacher's tone pauses.

N.B.: The pupil is permitted to represent the pauses by any combination of rest symbols except a chain of quarter-rests. Thus he
may write a 5-beat rest:

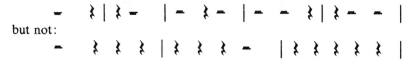

but not:

[187]

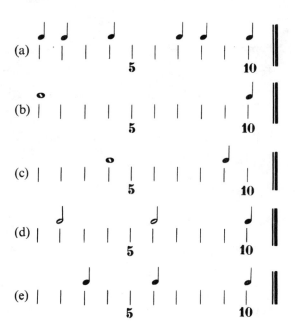

Add further exercises, if necessary.

DICTATION 4 ——

TEACHER: Tap the beats and sing tones of different pitch according to
the position of the notes.

PUPIL: Draw a line. Mark 10 beats below it. Write low, middle, and high
notes as you hear the tones sung, adding rests where necessary.

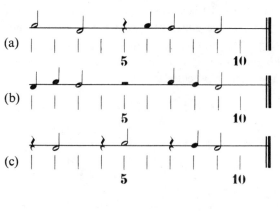

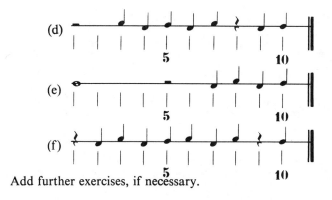

(d)

5   10

(e)

5   10

(f)

5   10

Add further exercises, if necessary.

CHAPTER II

DICTATION 5 ——

TEACHER: Tap the beats and play.
PUPIL: Write the rhythm of the played tones in notes and rests.

(1) To be written in $\frac{2}{4}$:

(a) $\frac{2}{4}$

(b) $\frac{2}{4}$

(c) $\frac{2}{4}$

(d) $\frac{2}{4}$

(e) $\frac{2}{4}$

(f) $\frac{2}{4}$

(2) To be written in $\frac{4}{4}$:

(a) $\frac{4}{4}$

(b) $\frac{4}{4}$

(c) $\frac{4}{4}$

(d) $\frac{4}{4}$

(e) $\frac{4}{4}$

(f) $\frac{4}{4}$

(g) $\frac{4}{4}$

DICTATION 6 ——

TEACHER: Sing, without tapping or counting.
PUPIL: Write, in notes and rests, the rhythm of the tones sung, in $\frac{4}{4}$.

(a) $\frac{4}{4}$

(b) $\frac{4}{4}$

(c) $\frac{4}{4}$

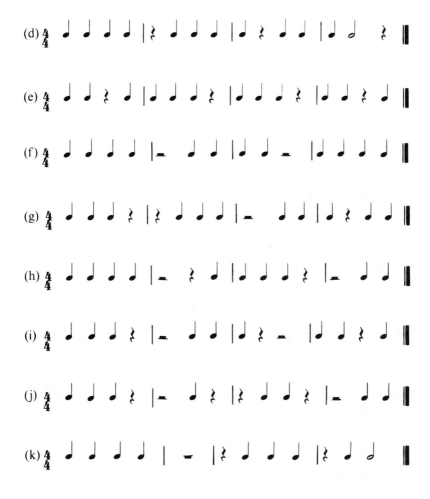

DICTATION 7 ——

(1) TEACHER: Sound the *a* with the fork. Play.
PUPIL: Write on staff-paper the tones sung by the teacher.

(2) TEACHER: Sound the *a*, sing.
   PUPIL: Same as before.

DICTATION 8 ———

(1) TEACHER: Play the melody (don't forget to sound the *a* first!) and tap the rhythm.
   PUPIL: Write down the melody, in $\frac{2}{4}$.

(2) TEACHER: Sing.
    PUPIL: Write down the melody in $\frac{4}{4}$.

DICTATION 9 —

(1) TEACHER: Sing, without tapping or counting (sound the *a*!), but
    announce the time-signature.
    PUPIL: Write down the melody.

Add further exercises, if necessary.

(2) TEACHER: Play, without tapping or counting.
PUPIL: Name the tones you hear.

CHAPTER III

DICTATION 10 ———

(1) TEACHER: Play, marking the beats. Announce the meter of each
example.
PUPIL: Write down the rhythm of the tones played.

(d)

(e)

(f)

(2) TEACHER: Sing; same conditions.
PUPIL: Write the rhythm.

(a)

(b)

(c)

(d)

(e)

(f)

[195]

DICTATION 11 ——

TEACHER: Sing, without marking the rhythm. Announce the meter and
give two beats in advance, in order to establish the tempo.
PUPIL: Write down the rhythm.

(a)

(b)

(c)

(d)

(e)

(f)

DICTATION 12 ——

(1) TEACHER: Play the following tones.
PUPIL: Write them down.

(2) TEACHER: Sing.
PUPIL: Write the notes.

(3) TEACHER: Sing.
    PUPIL: Name the tones.

(4) TEACHER: Name tones.
    PUPIL: Sing them.
    f, e, a, c, g, b, a, e, f, c, b, etc.

DICTATION 13 ———

(1) TEACHER: Sing and tap (or clap). Announce the meter and give
        preparatory beats.
    PUPIL: Write the melodies.

[197]

(2) TEACHER: Play and tap (or clap).
   PUPIL: Repeat, singing and tapping (or clapping).

CHAPTER IV

DICTATION 14 ——

(1) TEACHER: Sing and tap (or clap); announce the meter, and give
    preparatory beats.
    PUPIL: Write the rhythm of the tones sung.

(2) TEACHER: Play; same conditions.
    PUPIL: Write.

(d)

(e)

(3) TEACHER: Sing and tap (or clap).
   PUPIL: Repeat, singing and tapping (or clapping).

(a)

(b)

(c)

(d)

(e)

DICTATION 15 ——

(1) TEACHER: Sing. Announce the meter and clap (tap) the beats of one
   measure in advance; but do not beat while singing.
   PUPIL: Write down the rhythms.

(a)

(b)

(c)

(d)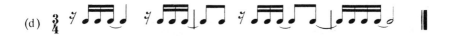

(2) TEACHER: Play; same conditions.
PUPIL: Clap the rhythms you have heard.

(a)

(b)

(c)

(d)

(3) TEACHER: Sing; same conditions.
PUPIL: Repeat, singing.

(a)

(b)

(c)

(d)

DICTATION 16 ——

(1) TEACHER: Play the following tones.
   PUPIL: Write them down.

(2) TEACHER: Sing.
   PUPIL: Write the notes.

(3) TEACHER: Sing.
   PUPIL: Name the tones.

(4) TEACHER: Name the tones.
   PUPIL: Sing them (men's voices sing in the lower octave).
   e', b', d', c', f', c'', d', g', a', e', c'', f', c', g', etc.

DICTATION 17 ——

(1) TEACHER: Sing, tapping (or clapping). Announce the meter, and
   give preparatory beats.
   PUPIL: Write the melody with the proper slurs and ties.
   la— la la la— etc.

(2) TEACHER: Sing; same conditions.
   PUPIL: Repeat, singing the melodies only.

[202]

DICTATION 18

TEACHER: Play, tapping (or clapping). Announce the meter and give
preparatory beats.
PUPIL: Write down the melody *and* the rhythm tapped (or clapped).

DICTATION 19

(1) TEACHER: Play, without marking the beats. Clap (tap) the beats of
one measure in advance without announcing the meter.
PUPIL: Write down the melody.

(2) TEACHER: Sing; same conditions.

PUPIL: Repeat, singing. Mark the first beat of every measure by clapping your hands.

CHAPTER V

DICTATION 20 ——

(1) TEACHER: Sing, tapping (or clapping). Announce the meter and give
      preparatory beats.
      PUPIL: Write the rhythm sung.

(2) TEACHER: Play and tap (or clap).
      PUPIL: Sing the played rhythm, tapping (or clapping).

(3) TEACHER: Sing, without marking the beats. Beat one measure in
      advance.
      PUPIL: Repeat singing. Clap the first beat of each measure.

(b) $\frac{3}{4}$ ♪ ♪ ♪. ♪ | ♫♫♫ ♪♫ ♪ ♪. | ♪♫ ♩ ‖

(c) $\frac{2}{4}$ ♪ ♪♩ ♪ | ♩. ♫ ♪ | ♫♫ ♫♫♫ | ♩ ♩ ‖

DICTATION 21 ——

(1) TEACHER: Name tones.
　　PUPIL: Write their letter-names, indicating which octave they belong
　　　to.
　　　e′, b′, a′, g″, c‴, f, e″, d′, b″, a′, g, etc.
(2) TEACHER: Play tones within the range *e—c‴* on the piano.
　　PUPIL: Name them.

　　For students with so-called "absolute pitch" this exercise will be no
problem. This does not mean that others cannot do it! The ear of every
normally gifted musician can be trained to become what is supposed to
be "absolute" in its judgment, the more so since there is no such abso-
luteness, based on any physical attribute of the ear. What is called "absolute pitch" is merely a highly developed ability to compare quickly an
audible impression with acoustic archetypes stored in our memory. These
archetypes are always taken from earlier musical experience and are
closely related to all kinds of external qualities of tones and of tone-
production. So the "absolute" ear of a violinist may depend on the
typical color of his instrument and its registers; when he hears tones in
other colors he unconsciously relates them to the familiar color-scale of
violin tones fixed in his memory through constant practice, and thus he
determines the pitch of the most recent tone impression. For a singer the
muscular tension of his vocal cords may be the basis of his judgment: he
measures the pitch of each tone he hears with the muscular effort he
would have to exert in producing it and thus finds its pitch.
　　Apart from experience, which time and again has proved that "absolute
pitch" can be acquired and developed, a simple reflection confirms the
relativity of even the most accurate tone-judgment: there is no absolute
standard of pitch! What we call *a* or *c* is merely by convention *a* or *c*, and
it has by no means a fixed place in the unlimited number of frequencies
in the audible range. Not only is a clarinet-player's *a* something very

[206]

different from the violinist's *a*, but either one varies considerably over a period of years. A certain tone may to-day be fixed at a level of 100 vibrations per second, but 20 years ago it may have had 105, and in 10 years it may have 97—our pitch in the last few decades has gone up about a half-tone! Judgments about the correspondence between pitches and tone-names cannot be more absolute than pitch itself, and consequently the question is merely how we can build up a fairly stable foundation for this judgment.

If the exercises in this book have been consistently performed in the way prescribed, this foundation is already to some degree established: the *a* of the tuning fork must by now be fixed in the pupil's mind, so that he can remember it whenever he hears another *a*. To further stabilize the feeling for this tone the teacher may from now on start each exercise with the instruction "Sing *a*," and then check this tone with the fork, instead of striking the fork first. This experiment may at first fail frequently enough, but after eighty or a hundred attempts a fairly firm and reproducible impression of *a* must be established. If not, the question may be raised whether there is any musical gift at all in a mind that cannot learn to remember and compare pitches.

The preceding exercise may be simplified for beginners: eliminate the great leaps, refer constantly to the *a* of the fork, and if necessary let each leap at first be approached stepwise from the fixed point *a*. Start each lesson with such an exercise in ear-training. And be patient!

DICTATION 22 ⸺

(1) TEACHER: Play the following melodies, and announce the keys into which the pupil is to change them. Beat one measure in advance.

PUPIL: Write them down; add missing accidentals to tones that have to be raised in order to obtain the keys marked at the beginning of each example.

in A major

in G major

in E major

in B major

in D major

(2) TEACHER: Sing, same conditions.
   PUPIL: Sing, correcting the tones that don't fit in the given tonality as they stand.

in D major

in A major

in B major

in G major

in E major

CHAPTER VI

Don't forget the Ear Training!
(see p. 206)

DICTATION 23 ——

(1) TEACHER: Sing and play alternately. Announce the meter, and tap (or clap).
   PUPIL: Write down the rhythm.

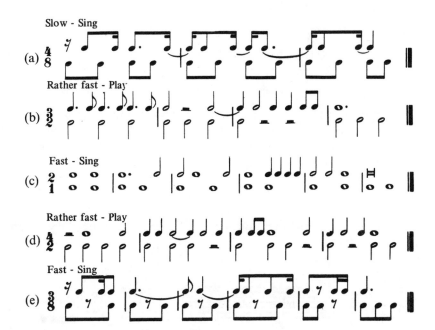

(2) TEACHER: Sing, without announcing the meter. Beat one measure in advance, then stop beating.

PUPIL: Write down the rhythm.

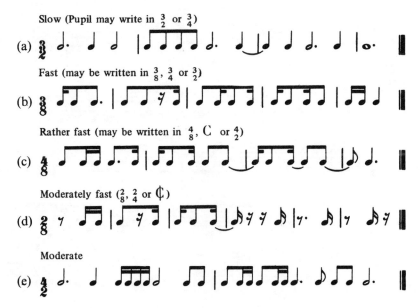

TEACHER: Name tones.
PUPIL: Write them down.

f''', g', b''', $e\sharp''$, $e\sharp$, a'', $a\sharp'''$, c'''', $c\sharp'$, g'', d''', $f\sharp''$, $g\sharp''''$, $b\sharp$, etc.

Some exercises in Ear Training using these high tones are to be recommended, but the degree to which such exercises can be undertaken must depend on the extent of the ability to recognize tones the pupil has gained thus far.

DICTATION 25 ——

TEACHER: Play. Announce the key and the meter. Beat only one measure in advance.
PUPIL: Write down.

(can be written in G ♭ major)

DICTATION 26 ——

(1) Same procedure as in Dictation 22, par. 1, page 207. Add flats to tones that have to be lowered.

in A♭ major

(a)

in E♭ major

(b)

in G♭ major   (Pupil can also write in F♯)

(c)

in D♭ major

(d)

in B♭ major

(e)

(2) Instructions: see Dictation 22, par. 2, page 208.

in F major

(a)

in D♭ major

(b)

in E♭ major

(c)

in A major

(d)

in F♯ major

(e)

CHAPTER VII

DICTATION 27 ——

(1) TEACHER: Sing* and play alternately. Announce the meter and mark the beats.

PUPIL: Write down the rhythm.

Rather slow - Sing

(a) $\frac{2}{4}$

Fast - Play

(b) $\frac{4}{2}$

Slow - Sing

(c) $\frac{3}{8}$

*The syllables la-la are apt to cause certain difficulties of articulation in fast succession. Use "da-da" or any other convenient syllables for this purpose.

Slow - Play

(d) $\frac{4}{8}$

Fast - Sing

(e) $\frac{3}{2}$

(3) TEACHER: Sing, without announcing the meter. Beat one measure
in advance; then stop beating.

PUPIL: Write down the rhythm.

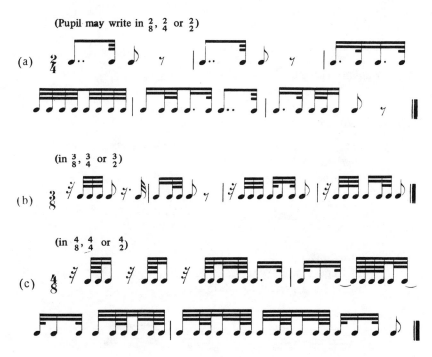

(Pupil may write in $\frac{2}{8}$, $\frac{2}{4}$ or $\frac{2}{2}$)

(a) $\frac{2}{4}$

(in $\frac{3}{8}$, $\frac{3}{4}$ or $\frac{3}{2}$)

(b) $\frac{3}{8}$

(in $\frac{4}{8}$, $\frac{4}{4}$ or $\frac{4}{2}$)

(c) $\frac{4}{8}$

[213]

(in $\frac{2}{8}$, $\frac{2}{4}$ or $\frac{2}{2}$)

(d)

(in $\frac{2}{2}$ or $\frac{2}{4}$)

(e)

DICTATION 28 ——

TEACHER: Name tones.
PUPIL: Write them down in bass clef.

> *g′ F♯, b, B♭, a′, C♯, C♭, c♯, c♭, b♯, c′, d♭, d♭′, E, e′,* etc

Ear-Training: TEACHER: Play tones in bass region.
PUPIL: Name them.

DICTATION 29 ——

(1) TEACHER: Play a given tone (marked ○) and sing another one
    (marked ●).
    PUPIL: Name the interval between the two tones.

(2) TEACHER: Sing.
    PUPIL: Repeat what you have heard, but sing it a perfect fifth
    higher (or a perfect fourth lower).

(a)

(3) TEACHER: Sing.
   PUPIL: Repeat. Sing a perfect fourth higher (or a perfect fifth lower).

(e)

DICTATION 30 ——

(1) TEACHER: Play, without beating except for one measure in advance. Announce the meter.

PUPIL: Write the melody in $\mathcal{9}$:

Moderately fast

(a)

Fast

(b)

Andante

(c)

Rather fast

(d)

(2) TEACHER: Sing. Announce the meter, and the two keys. No beating.
PUPIL: Sing what you heard, but add or omit accidentals so as to
change the key as directed.

CHAPTER VIII

DICTATION 31 ——

TEACHER: Name the following notes.
PUPIL: Write them down in 𝄢:

,B e C♯ C♭ ,C♯ ,,A ,,B♯ ,C A♭ b♯ c' ,E ,F♭ ,D♯ ,G♭ etc.

[217]

(1) TEACHER: Play the lower tone, sing the higher one, then vice versa.
   PUPIL: Name the intervals you hear.

(2) TEACHER: Play.
   PUPIL: Name the intervals.

(3) TEACHER: Play similar examples, but don't use intervals larger than
      an octave.
   PUPIL: Try to name the tones of the intervals.

Whether the pupil can succeed in this exercise depends entirely on the
degree of perfection in hearing obtained by the earlier exercises in ear-
training. If it appears that the pupil's ear is not sufficiently developed yet
to master this example, more preparatory exercises have to be inserted.

DICTATION 33 ——

TEACHER: Play the following lines. Announce meter and key. Beat one
   measure in advance, if necessary.
PUPIL: Listen at first to the soprano line, till you know it, then do the
   same with the bass. Write them both down as one single two-part
   piece.

CHAPTER IX

DICTATION 34 ——

TEACHER: Play. Announce the meter, beat one measure in advance.
PUPIL: Find the key. Write down.

DICTATION 35 —

(1) TEACHER: Play the lower tone, sing the upper one; then vice versa.
    PUPIL: Name the intervals you hear.

(2) TEACHER: Play.
   PUPIL: Name the intervals.

(3) TEACHER: Play fifths, fourths, thirds, sixths, seconds, and sevenths,
    suiting the order of succession, choice of register, and tempo to
    the pupils' ability.
   PUPIL: Name the tones of each interval.

DICTATION 36 ——

TEACHER: Play the following two-part examples. Count one measure in
    advance. Announce key and meter.
PUPIL: Write them down.

[222]

More dictation material for this exercise and the corresponding ones in the next two chapters can easily be found in short sections of all kinds of published music.

CHAPTER X

DICTATION 37 ——

TEACHER: Sing: announce key and meter; do not beat time.
PUPIL: Sing, clapping the first beat of each measure.

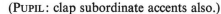
(Pupil: clap subordinate accents also.)

(c)

(Pupil: same as before.)

(d)

(e) Fast

(f)

DICTATION 38 ——

TEACHER: Name tones.
PUPIL: Write them down in alto clef.

$c\sharp$, e'', $f\sharp'$, $a\flat$, c', $b\sharp$, $e\flat$, $c\flat$, $b\flat$, g'', $e\sharp$, f'', f, $g\sharp$, etc

DICTATION 39 ——

TEACHER: Play intervals.
PUPIL: Write the sound you hear in all diminished and augmented forms
you can find. Thus you may hear:

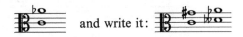

Write in alto clef.

DICTATION 40 ——

TEACHER: Play on the piano. Announce key and meter.
PUPIL: Sing at first the middle voice of each three-part setting in the
octave convenient to your voice. Then sing the lower voice. Finally
write the whole piece down. Write the upper line in alto clef.

[226]

CHAPTER XI

DICTATION 41 ——

TEACHER: Name tones.
PUPIL: Write them in tenor clef.

f, $b\sharp$, c', $g\flat'$, $e\sharp$, $b\flat\flat'$, $d\flat'$, $d\sharp$, $a\times'$, $a\flat\flat$, $B\sharp$, c'', $f\flat'$, $c\flat$, etc.

DICTATION 42 ——

TEACHER: Play the following intervals.
PUPIL: Write down what you hear in all possible doubly augmented and
doubly diminished forms, in tenor clef.

DICTATION 43 ——

TEACHER: Play. Announce key and meter.
PUPIL: Sing first each of the two middle voices. Then write down each
    complete example. Use tenor and alto clefs wherever possible (for
    both upper and lower staves).

(j)

INDEX

Abbreviations (in notation), 168 ff.
"Absolute pitch," 206 f.
Accent, 43, 93 f., 97 ff., 116a. 136 f., 155
Accidentals, 53 f., 67, 70 f., 164; ✕ , ♭♭,
   145
   See also Flat, Natural sign, Sharp,
   etc.
   See also Key-signature
Aeolian mode, 165
Alla breve, 62
Alteration, *see* Chromatic alteration
Alto clef, 142
Ambitus, 164
Analysis, 157
Arpeggiando, arpeggio, 171
Arsis, 94
Articulation, 39, 172
Augmentation dot, 30, 45 f., 65, 115,
   116a double, 77
Augmented intervals, *see* Intervals

Bar, 9
Bar-line, 9, 94, 99, 136 f.
   auxiliary, 136 f.
   See also Double bar
Bass clef, 82 f., 85
Bassoon (sometimes uses tenor clef),
   159
Beams, 17 f., 23, 31 f., 38, 46, 77, 120,
   136 f., 169 ff.
   in bipartite meters, 17 f., 46
   in irregular meters, 136 f.
   in tripartite meters, 31 f., 46
   in vocal music, 38
Beats, accented, 93 f.
   irregular divisions of, 115 ff., 120 f.
   metric, 4
   unaccented, 93 f.
Bipartite division of tripartite note-
   values, 116a
Bis, 170
Bowing, 39, 172
Brevis, 65

C-clef, 142, 159 f.
   See also Alto clef, Mezzo-soprano
      clef, Soprano clef, Tenor clef
'Cello (sometimes uses tenor clef), 159
Chord, 86
Chromatic alteration, 53 f., 131, 145,
   148 f., 175

Chromatic half-tone, 53, 67, 145
Chromatic scale, 175
Church modes, 163 ff.
Circle of fifths (fourths), 146 f., 164
Clefs, 12, 51, 82 f., 142, 159 f., 174
   See also names of individual clefs
Comma, 144
Compound metric patterns, 98 ff.,
   115 ff., 136 f.
Conducting patterns, 94 f., 102 ff., 112,
   121, 137
Contra octave, 106

Da capo, 71, 81
Dal segno, 71
D. C., *see* Da capo
Decuplets, 116b
Degree, 58, 84
   in chromatic scale, 175
Diatonic half-tone, 53, 67, 149, 175
Diatonic scale, 58, 174 f.
Diminished intervals, *see* Intervals
Divisions of the beat, irregular, *see*
   Beats
Dominant, 58, 84, 131, 175
Dominant, model, *see* Repercussa
Dorian mode, 163 ff.
Dot, *see* Augmentation dot, Staccato
Dotted notes and rests, *see* Augmenta-
   tion dot
Double bar, heavy, final, 5
   light, sectional, 13
Double bass (sometimes uses tenor
   clef), 159
Double dot (augmentation), 77
Double flat, 145 f.
Double sharp, 145 f.
Doubly augmented and diminished in-
   tervals, *see* Intervals
D. S. (Dal segno), 71
Duplets, 116a
Dynamic accent, *see* Accent
Dynamics (indications), 130, 155 f.
Eighth-note, -rest, 17, 20; dotted, 46
Eleventh (interval), 161
Embellishments, 170 ff.
Enharmonic equivalence, 144, 146 ff.,
   175
Equal temperament, 52, 144, 147
Expression (indications), 62f., 78,
   129 f., 155 f.

Accents:

>   43
∧   43
!   172
–   172

Accidentals:

♯   53 f., 70 f., 145
♭   67, 70 f., 145
𝄪   145 f.
♭♭   145 f.
♮   53, 71, 145

Articulation, Bowing:

•   172
⌢··   172
⊓   172
∨   172

Clefs:

 160

  12, 51

  160

  160

  142

Clefs—*Continued*

 159

  160

  82 f., 85

  160

 159 f.

  159 f.

Ornaments:

∿   171
∿   171
∾   171 f.
∽   172

Time-signatures:

$\frac{3}{8}$ 62
$\frac{4}{8}$ 62
$\frac{6}{8}$ 100
$\frac{9}{8}$ 100
$\frac{12}{8}$ 100

Time-signatures—*Continued*			Miscellaneous:	
$\frac{2}{4}$	9		ᱍ	17
$\frac{3}{4}$	30 ff.		⹀	65
$\frac{4}{4}$	9		⌒	13, 95
C	9		*8va*	66, 106
¢	62			
$\frac{6}{4}$	100		⌐1. ⌐2.	70
$\frac{2}{2}$	62		⊕	71, 81
$\frac{3}{2}$	62, 65		𝄊	71, 81
$\frac{4}{2}$	62, 65			

For further time-signatures see Time-signatures less usual than those listed individually